TOXIC JESUS

A JOURNEY FROM HOLY SHIT TO SPIRITUAL HEALING

MARC-HENRI SANDOZ PARADELLA

APOCRYPHILE
PRESS

Apocryphile Press
1700 Shattuck Ave #81
Berkeley, CA 94709
www.apocryphilepress.com

Copyright © 2020 by Marc-Henri Sandoz Paradella
Printed in the United States of America
ISBN 978-1-949643-70-1 | paperback
ISBN 978-1-949643-71-8 | ePub

CONTENTS

FOREWORD

We met in a legendary land known as the heart chakra of the Earth. I remember it clearly with his radiant smile and compassionate gaze. There was something about this man that spoke volumes in the spaces of silence between words with a gentle power emanating from his being. I felt a spontaneous joy in meeting Marc-Henri, and this would be the beginning of bearing witness to a deeply heroic journey. Fast forward to the following year in Italy, where he commenced a yoga teacher training with me on two legs but would graduate with only one leg.

This is a story of healing, liberation, and fierce embrace. It is a call to action to face our fears and turn toward our pain, so we can free ourselves from the hidden forces that keep us in denial and shut us down to the real power of love. The intention of this book is to help us heal from toxic spirituality, wash away the layers of guilt and shame, and bring us into profound connection with the Divine. By no means is this an easy journey, which is why we need a skillful and empathetic guide who has traversed the underworld, spelunked the darkest caves, and emerged triumphant to now lead the way.

Marc-Henri grew up with a sincere love and devotion for Jesus. He became a pastor in an evangelical church for fifteen years, was swept away in the currents of fanaticism and dogmatism, began to question the sectarianism of his faith, and eventually left his position of leadership within the church. As a result, he lost his entire social network, went through a painful divorce, and faced the dark night of the soul. All the while, he persistently confronted his own conditioned thinking and toxic beliefs, explored other spiritual traditions, became a meditation teacher and counselor, found his true beloved Evelise, turned to shadow work, and connected in true intimacy with emotions that had been estranged, denied and shut down from childhood trauma.

Upon discovering a rare cancer in his left leg, his only hope for survival was a full amputation up to the hip joint. In the midst of his darkest hours before the amputation, he was guided back to Jesus in an authentic spiritual experience. He bravely underwent the surgery, returned to the yoga training even as he was learning to walk with a prosthetic leg, and inspired each of us immeasurably. We all wept with grief for his amputated leg and we intensely celebrated the gift of his life. In some ways, the journey of Marc-Henri was just beginning and as he "cleaned up the dark part of his religious heritage" and opened to a powerful new force awakening in him.

The journey of this book is a radical alchemy of transforming what Marc-Henri refers to as the "toxic Jesuses" into a life-sustaining spirituality. The toxic Jesuses are born out of oppressive systems that manipulate, control, and guilt-trip the practitioner. This is his story of identifying and dismantling each form of toxicity in his beliefs, mind, and body. As a result of his own brave work, he is capable of guiding us to ask the really tough questions, lean into discomfort, and dismantle toxic spirituality that lives within us. As we deconstruct our own toxic identities with honest inquiry, we are ultimately uplifted with expansive energy that frees us from our own pain and suffering.

This is a very real and vulnerable account of one man's journey with Jesus. Through his own confrontation with trauma, toxicity, and abuse, he unpacks a pathway for identifying harmful spirituality and awakening with authentic spirituality. He urges us to reclaim our inner strength and resiliency, face our shadows, and cultivate a nontoxic relationship with the divine. In doing so, we become more deeply human and begin to heal the wounded, fragmented parts of ourselves. We become increasingly free of oppressive beliefs and come to live a life of joy and shared humanity.

In the unveiling of the toxic Jesuses, which is another way of saying toxic spirituality, the author discovered what he knew all along—the power of an ancient wisdom, the truth of grace, and the spacious opening in the heart to embrace the whole of life. Toxic spirituality perpetuates harm, covers up the wounds, spiritually bypasses, hides the truth, avoids facing reality, and rejects the pain. But the movement from toxic spirituality to healthy spirituality embraces the innermost being and allows for honest showing up and true, deep connection with self and other.

The benefits of healthy spirituality are boundless with a renewal of life force energy, greater receptivity and intuition, increased confidence, healing body shame, emotional literacy with the full spectrum of emotions, more resourcefulness to navigate challenges, and being more in touch with our infinite self. Who doesn't want all this and more? In this journey from "holy shit to spiritual healing," we are gifted with increased clarity and growing courage to confront toxic spirituality and walk away from it. We become more intimate with our own hidden pain so that we can heal and grow, flourish and thrive. As we become more dedicated to healing our traumas and wounds—instead of denying, defending, or justifying them—

we begin to live our lives in a way of nourishment and integration, and calling home the marginalized places within our own being. We reclaim our power, face our shadows, and rest more within the great mystery.

As a storyteller, I relate deeply to the hero/heroine's journey and to the quest of the innermost self. Marc-Henri and I met in the legendary land of Avalon, the Isle of Apples, a mystical place in Somerset, England, known as Glastonbury. In myth and legend, the wounded King Arthur was taken to the healing Isle of Avalon where he also received the famous sword Excalibur gifted to him out of the watery depths by the Lady of the Lake. This mystical land also holds the legends of Joseph of Arimathea, the uncle of Jesus, who was said to have carried his pilgrim's staff and the Holy Grail to these lands after the death of Jesus. Christian mythology says this is the very place where he hid the chalice of the last supper beneath the water and henceforth, they flowed forth with healing grace and renewal. In this land known as the heart chakra of the Earth, there's a beauty in the tapestry of all our stories, and the most sacred return to the heart and the power of real love.

This book is a powerful invitation to say yes to the whole of life and live in authentic connection with deep, true spirituality. May each reader feel inspired to do the work and show up fully for real transformation that serves the greater whole, It is my great honor to write these words in support of Marc-Henri, an amazing soul who has paved the way for many to reclaim their spirituality in a healthy, luminous way.

Saprema,

Sianna Sherman

Founder & Visionary of the *Rasa Yoga Collective* and *Alchemy of Avalon*

Topanga, CA – July 20, 2020, New Moon in Cancer

INTRODUCTION

AN UNEXPECTED NEW PERSPECTIVE

Why do I find myself in Oregon in July, 2018, at the age of 54, taking part in a long-planned intensive-therapy group, exploring with nine other people the depth of our emotions, grief and inner sufferings? Why, only six weeks after the amputation of my entire left leg due to a rare cancer, did I decide to come here, despite a twelve-hour flight from my home and not yet having fully recovered from major surgery. Why, lying on the ground, surrounded by my fellow participants and by two very skilled therapists, am I crying in deep despair like I never have in my entire life, yelling my grief and anger for my lost leg, shouting that I want to live, that I have suffered too much in this life? Finally, why am I exclaiming that I don't need Jesus, just me?

These thoughts and this book were born in that group, when I discovered a part of me that I wasn't suspecting—a part that had suffered so much that it hardly wanted to live; a part that had stayed frozen in the experiences and beliefs of a child who had reason to feel traumatized and abused.

As a child I had been trapped in a system of beliefs that were deeply ingrained in my family. This system left me hardly any chance to grow and live a happy and healthy life. The beliefs were all built around the figure of Jesus: Jesus the healer, Jesus who was supposed to intervene from above, Jesus who sacrificed himself for our sins and wanted our faith and adoration, and so much more.

As an adult, I'm now ready to connect with this child. I began to listen to his painful, hidden story. I felt his despair, sadness, grief and anger. I discovered which of those repressed feelings had turned into darker and even more deeply hidden undercurrents—among them hatred and fear of life, compulsion to self-sacrifice and self-sabotage, distrust and disgust for himself and everyone else, and a pervading terror.

Connecting to him and to all of that suffering, I felt compassion for him. I could understand him. I could listen to his beliefs, to his needs, to his longings. All of it was such a part of me. Actually, it *was* me.

I decided to be with that child unconditionally every day of my life. I decided to speak for him too, and to address the abuse and mistreatment he had to endure.

In so doing I felt him somewhat relieved, a bit more trusting. What he needed was a loving and caring adult, mature enough to stay with him and to empathize with what he had been through, to acknowledge his feelings and help him express them, to lovingly confront his toxic shames, compulsions and beliefs, to be his loving companion, allowing him to heal and to build a whole new way of relating to life. I could be and would be that adult. I owed it to him and to myself.

This book is the story of me speaking for him. At the same time it's the story of my journey with Jesus and the story of my life. It's a story in which true grace and love for the divine coexist with tons of what I call holy shit and a lot of spiritual abuse. Faith may be a beautiful part of a healthy life, giving grounding and perspective, sustaining life and love. Unfortunately, faith can also manifest as a range of toxic beliefs, well hidden behind attractive ideas, creeds and discourses that nonetheless infect all parts of the psyche, torturing and even slowly killing the soul.

This happens especially when faith is built on unhealed wounds, ones we are barely conscious of, when it meets a history of mistreatments and abuses that are hard to face.

That's what happened in my parents' life. They were both full of deep wounds, hidden anxieties and extreme vulnerabilities. But their desire to escape them and convince themselves of their strengths and abilities severely handicapped them in fostering a healthy life for me and my sister. Since early childhood, we were deprived of the means to go through the normal phases of development and growth.

My Early Years

I was raised with Jesus. I had no question about his existence or how to relate to him. The only possible (allowed) question was whether I had done enough according to the Bible's demands and God's exigencies. I've been bathed, even soaked, since my very first years of life in the evocation of his person. I've been plunged into the reading of the Bible since childhood. I've identified with him. I've explored many facets of his person and of the ways he and his message and actions have been understood and used and abused. He has been my imaginary friend as well as a poignant absence, my oppressor as well as my liberator, my abuser as well as my comforter, and so many other things.

I remember the torment I felt at seven years of age, thinking that if I hadn't testified enough to my school friends, they would eventually go to hell. And I would be the one responsible.

Around the same age I remember falling in love with a girl in my school and asking my mother if I was allowed to kiss her. The answer was that kissing was something reserved for married people. Beyond just hearing the words, I felt a visceral discomfort and inexplicable shame. I then concluded that somehow being in love with that little girl was bad and that I had to stay away from those feelings—and if possible, from girls at the same time.

I remember at fifteen wanting to go to a band concert: Dire Straits. My father explained that even if I was strong enough to go to such an event, it would be a bad example for weaker people and would eventually drive some of them to fall into temptation, from drugs to sex outside marriage, to worshipping the devil, all the things that were encouraged by that kind of music. I didn't buy it. I went to the concert anyway, in an attempt to gain some freedom, to rebel against what I had begun to feel was an abuse of authority. It was a great concert and a great memory to this day. But I paid a high price, enduring feelings of guilt every time I tried to put off that yoke and gain some autonomy.

I remember, too, professing my love to Jesus, giving my life to him many times in various church meetings, from the age of four to sixteen. (You're never sure if it's done completely and properly, so when some guilt or fear is awakened by a skilled preacher, you proclaim the Lord again, just in case.) I stopped doing that after my baptism at sixteen, the external form of the ritual having somehow a reassuring effect, not depending completely on me and on my own faith and good inner disposition.

I remember moments of extreme loneliness (many of them) and sometimes (only rarely, I must say) finding comfort by invoking Jesus's loving and caring presence.

Most of all, and on a happier note, I remember my church's youth group. There, from the age of fourteen, I found something I was cruelly missing: connection with other kids my age, females and males, and the authorization, inner and outer, to relate with them and enjoy their company. I also found the father/big brother figure I was longing for in the person of the pastor. This group became my tribe, my friends, my family, my life purpose. We spent most of our weekends at the home of one of my friends, where he had a big garden and a ping-pong table. Going to church became much more attractive, because it was an occasion to meet and to sit together.

The group became the center of my life, my salvation, my refuge from the lonesome, dark shadow, a persistent feeling of anxiety every time I was at home. I remember lying in my bed at night, praying to Jesus that this group may continue to exist, because I needed it to survive. And I truly meant it.

I soon became part of the group leadership team, organizing camps with the pastor, learning to speak in public, testifying about Jesus, going to hospitals to sing Christian songs and propose praying with the patients. Most of all, I spent as much time away from my home as possible, favoring instead those people I felt closer to and connected with.

It was paradise, except for when I wasn't in church or with them. Then I found myself again facing the hell of my loneliness, anxiety and despair, struggling with the reminders of those parts of my humanity I tried so hard to repress. I had to repress them, I thought, to allow myself and others to think I was a good Christian. Among forbidden traits, I had to hide my sexuality: I remember many times sneaking into a porno movie cinema, under age, trying to satisfy the curiosity and compulsions of an adolescent full of hormones. Of course, I paid later with days of guilt and feeling like shit. I was angry, too. I remember many fights with my father, fueled by the same hormones, no doubt, but also by the true recognition that there was something wrong with the way he saw himself—so wise, discerning, and full of spiritual authority. Every time, I paid for those attempts at some freedom and autonomy with guilt, still more guilt, and resolutions and promises to God that I would behave better.

My Later Years, and Intimations of Grace

Finally, during my college years—perhaps you can see it coming—I realized I had to become a pastor. I decided to study theology at the University of Geneva. The choice disappointed and worried my father because the faculty was not evangelical, but he decided I was strong enough in my faith to face those hardly believing protestants and remain a true Christian. So I went through those studies. I faced questions and doubts about my narrow view of Christianity, and felt aspirations to a wider and freer practice of spirituality emerge, as well as a wider and freer life in general. I could only overcome these tests, as I saw them, by an increase in rigidity and a kind of fanaticism in my religious zeal. I went on to become a leader of the youth group and then a part-time junior pastor in another evangelical church, where I became co-pastor when my studies were successfully completed.

The picture may seem dark and sad at this point. And it is. Yet, when I remember the kid I was, the adolescent, the young man, when I connect with each one of them still living inside me, I find something very sincere and alive in all of them. Along with the guilt, the repressed feelings and denied vital impulses, I can see a true love for the divine, an attraction to the mystery, a desire to dive deep inside myself.

Grace was present all along the way—that at least it seems clear to me now—but not where I thought it should have been. Present in a soft and discrete way. Present in the love I was receiving in my dear youth group. Present in my attempts to implement autonomy and growth, even at the price of guilt and shame. Present in my decision to study in a place where my system of thought and belief would be confronted at least a little and where I would be invited to become more adult and spacious. I could feel this grace when I preached about a loving and welcoming God, sustaining life and promoting freedom, as

I discovered and shared parts of the Bible that expressed those profound truths, and when I prayed for people and felt deeply how much they were loved.

I could feel this grace when I was holding my newborn babies, first my daughter and then, two years later, my son, and feeling the preciousness of their presence in this world, and their need for care and love.

Later, many years later, grace manifested in sustaining my decision to begin psychotherapy, when I faced the fact that I was profoundly unhappy, feeling empty inside despite all my faith and piety, and trapped in a dysfunctional and destructive relationship with my former wife. I felt grace when I decided to resign from my job as a pastor and began to look for a regular job. I remember feeling a clear impression of Jesus telling me he was with me and that he wanted me to grow and not to hold his hand all the time anymore. I felt grace, surprisingly, when I faced the loneliness and disappointment of seeing that my friendships and relationships, all built around the church in one way or another, had just vanished over a brief period of time. I sometimes felt it through the years that followed, years characterized by doubts, agnosticism, semi-depression and the struggle to find my place in the society outside the walls of the church and adapt to jobs that were much less rewarding and interesting than my former pastoral activity. I felt grace when I finally decided to divorce, after more than twenty years of a difficult and hurtful marriage, despite all of the efforts and sometimes love invested by both parties to try to save it. I felt grace most profoundly when I met the smart and beautiful woman Evelise, who has become my wife.

I was conscious of the presence of grace when I discovered meditation and yoga, when I met people of other spiritual traditions beyond my narrow conception of Christianity and could honor and recognize the depth of their practice and love for the divine.

Finally and unexpectedly, I felt grace in a dramatic way two months before I began to write this book, when I heard the cruel diagnosis of a rare, malignant bone cancer that cost me my entire left leg and still makes my long-term survival uncertain to this day. My wife and I, each in different ways, had the intuition to reconnect with Jesus in this difficult moment and to open up to his helping and healing energy. I then experienced, to my immense surprise, completely unexpected moments of peace and confidence, especially in the midst of the darkest hours before my amputation.

So I continued the group therapy in Oregon. In it, I've had the opportunity to discover a way to truly listen to my inner world, following a technique called shadow work. It's a challenging and delicate practice, but an incredibly efficient and respectful way of inner exploration, freeing and healing.

In engaging deeper into shadow work, I began to listen to the child, teenager, and young adult I had been. I discovered their hidden wounds, until now impossible to express as sadness, anger, desires. I connected with them. I felt more and more compassion and love for them. As a result, I began to reconcile with myself and become more and more integrated. I considered parts of myself that had been for so long a deserted no-man's land, and I allowed them to be part of me again. I recognized they had always been part of me and deserved to be cared for. I listened to their stories. I could understand what they were feeling. I could share their sadness, anger, fears. Despite all their suffering, and with the help of my therapist, my wife and my colleagues in the therapy group, the adult I am now could begin to take care and to open a safe space for healing and peace for all those wounded parts of me.

Giving that precious gift to myself, I began to discover unsuspected parts of my humanity, new depths of feelings, a new freedom of sensibility and intuition. I could feel more and more confident, more in touch with my true, beautiful and wounded self.

Along the way, I began to discover that the Jesus imprinted in the depth of me, the Jesus I had served and adored, this Jesus had many faces. And many of those faces were dark and toxic. In my long journey with Jesus, I had been intimate with him, but I discovered that much of that intimacy was with those toxic Jesuses.

What I mean by toxic Jesuses are those conceptions of Jesus that exist and grow in the space between our inner wounds, from the places where we have been neglected or abused. These Jesuses are born in the repressed expectations of the wounded child within many of us. They are born in the tyranny and oppressive systems that have emerged to cover and exploit those wounds.

The toxic Jesuses attract the worship and dedication of those of us who have been severely wounded and need a way to avoid facing it. Too much of what happens in churches owes something to those sad and life oppressing dynamics, even when—and fortunately it happens often—the oppression coexists with an amount of true love for the divine.

The more I unveiled these toxic Jesuses in my own history, the more anger and even rage I felt against them. That's when this book became necessary. I owe it to myself, I owe it to those who have been oppressed and tyrannized within me. And I owe it to others who have been or who are still confronted with teachings and practices in churches or religious groups that work subtly or grossly against life, against freedom, against joy, growth and intelligence.

Unfortunately, there are many such teachings, deliberate or not, in and out of every kind of Christian church or religious group: Evangelicals, Catholics, Jehovah's Witnesses, Mormons, Christian Scientists, Yogis, Buddhists, Muslims, Spiritualists. The list goes on.

Yet in this unveiling, I began to discover another face of Jesus—a new face that I paradoxically knew from the beginning, one that was usually hidden by the noise and arrogant claims of the toxic ones. This new face is bright and full of light, spacious, life-affirming, and much gentler, not trying to impose itself. It waits patiently, in the margins and in the silence, sustaining life and expecting it to grow, seemingly weak but possessing ancient wisdom and power.

This face of Jesus I want to talk about, too, and I also owe it to myself and others. But to do that, I must begin by talking about all the toxic Jesuses I had to confront in my own history. During my inner work I discovered that they are present in the whole history of the Church, even in the Bible, and certainly in many of the messages and practices today in which the name of Jesus is invoked. Under other names they can be found in any religious group.

These are the toxic Jesuses I discovered in my inner world:

- Jesus the negator, who wants us to dismiss our own experience, feelings and intelligence.
- Jesus the punisher, who loves death and wants sacrifice and suffering.
- Jesus the magician, who expects things to come from above and wants us to do the same.
- Jesus the castrator, who makes humans small and disempowered.
- Jesus the oppressor, who gives power to tyrants.
- Jesus the misogynist, who hates and oppresses women.
- Jesus the patriarchalist, who promotes every system of domination.
- Jesus the enabler, who covers abuses.
- Jesus the fanatic, who supports extremism and violence.

- Jesus the Puritan, who despises human experience and pleasure.
- Jesus the pure spirit, disincarnate and antisexual.
- Jesus Frankenstein, who gives birth to monsters.

I'll devote some pages to each one of them in this book. I'll show how they have oppressed me, how they are oppressing many, how they are born of and feed on unresolved wounds and hidden fear and shame. I'll also show how to find freedom from them, how to find the courage and strength to confront them and send them away—what you might call a Jesus exorcism.

By unveiling the toxic ones, another Jesus will naturally emerge in the last part of our book.

PART I

THE TOXIC JESUSES

HOLY SHIT AND SPIRITUAL ABUSE

If you bring forth what is within you,
What you bring forth will save you.
If you do not bring forth what is within you,
What you do not bring forth will destroy you.
—words attributed to Jesus, Gospel of Thomas

1

JESUS THE NEGATOR

First, an introductory vignette:

At nine years old, my leg breaks almost spontaneously when I fall on the ground while running to escape a girl my age with whom I had been fighting.

The doctors say that my femur is extremely fragile due to a rare genetic disease. I have to spend months in the hospital, go through long and delicate surgery to repair my bone with pieces of steel and screws. At eleven, I undergo a new surgery to remove them, and then receive orthopedic care to correct problems in my growth caused by the surgeries.

I have become lame. I have to wear special shoes, one with an horrible thick compensating sole. I must be overly cautious about anything that could cause a shock and break my leg again, unable to practice any sport. I'm overweight and full of nervous tics.

So at twelve years old, my father comes to speak to me very seriously. He wears his solemn/angry/concentrated/spiritual face. I feel flattered by the rare attention. He tells me that a renowned spiritual healer is coming for a healing and revival meeting in the church we attend. His "speciality" is healing and fixing unequal legs. My father wants me to attend the meeting and receive a healing, but for that I need to be ready. I need to have faith, because that's what Jesus wants to enable the healing.

My answer is "okay." I'm going to pray and prepare myself very seriously, and I strongly believe that Jesus can and will heal me through his servant, the healer. And I do that. During the two months before the coming of the healer, I pray every day to thank Jesus that he's going to heal me. I read my Bible with an increased dedication.

My father invests his own faith in the project, too, writing letters to every member of our family to announce the healing, which is going to happen for sure. Most of them aren't Evangelical Christians, or Christians at all, but the idea is to bring them to an inescapable witnessing of the grace and power of Jesus. I remember him showing me answers from some of them trying to dissuade him from foolishness, concerned by the impact it could have on me if that healing failed. He replies that he is completely assured of the grace and love of Jesus and has nothing to fear.

My mother follows submissively, but her passivity probably hides mistrust, as for any idea not originated in herself or by any of her temporarily elected figures of admiration. In any case, she expresses nothing against the glorious hope of healing her son's painful condition and at least keeps her position as the neutral witness in this situation of abuse.

My little sister also doesn't say a word, as usual. But she expresses her uneasiness with recurrent stomachaches, lack of appetite, mutism.

The day arrives. The revival meeting happens tonight.

We enter the church, a solemn family arriving for a divine encounter. The healer begins his service with a very long sermon about God's love in Jesus, who wants to bless and heal us all, but most of all save us. He sweats, jumps around, gesticulates. You can see his sincerity and true dedication in the energy, spluttering, and persuasion that emanate from him. The audience is conquered. Then comes the call to give your life to Jesus, which I answer quickly, to be really sure it's well and completely done, then the call to healing. The healer makes me come in front of the crowd and sit on a chair, where he shows everybody the evident difference in my leg lengths. Then he kneels in front of me, holding both my heels, and begins to pray.

I concentrate to the utmost and expect to experience something strong coming from God as he prays. I imagine and hope for a kind of spiritual high, an ecstasy, a feeling of love and plenitude, a face-to-face with Jesus. So of course I'm disappointed not to feel anything except maybe a little heat in my legs as the healer holds them and moves them and pulls them strongly towards his lap. But who would dare to judge or criticize the way God acts? Not me for sure. He calls on Jesus with enthusiasm and shows the crowd how my legs move and how their lengths are normalizing. So anyway, the healing happens, even without any strong feeling of the divine. I come back to my chair, noting the long, enthusiastic applause of the believing throng. I try hard to keep my faith solid, because people who doubt their healing may lose it. So said the healer.

Only one formality remains: going to the doctor to make an official ascertainment of my newly healthy condition. An appointment was made long ago with that intention. My mother takes me there; my father has to work. The doctor measures my legs with a kind of sad expression on his face, sadder still when he looks at my mother and says that nothing has changed: I'm still lame and there's no sign that my frailty and genetic disease have abated.

I just remember being blank at that moment, a sense of my head emptying of everything: blood, thoughts, sensations, emotions.

We go back home. My father returns from the gymnasium he directs. My mother underscores the doctor's atheism and skepticism and expresses doubts about the way he measured my leg. My father calls the pastor of the church where the healer is lodging. Don't worry, says the healer. In difficult cases, you often have to ask twice for healing. Keep faith, don't lose your healing. Fortunately there is another meeting that evening in another city not too far away.

Up we go. The preaching. The call to give your life to Jesus. The call to healing. The chair. The prayers. The enthusiasm. The legs moving under the hands of the healer. The applause.

And down we go. The appointment with the doctor the day after. The sad expression. The disappointment.

Again, I'm honored by an encounter with my father. With his same solemn/angry/concentrated/spiritual expression, he looks at me and explains: we all have to keep faith. The healing is going to come, only in another way. God knows what he does.

My mother again stays silent, seemingly approving and keeping behind a closed face any possible doubt or inner conflict. My sister keeps holding back any words, suffering recurrently from her stomachaches and beginning to hide as much as she can strange behavior concerning food and assorted anxieties. She would be diagnosed much later as schizophrenic, in her late thirties, after years of suffering and many difficult episodes.

I keep trying hard to believe. Two days after those sad events, I'm in church. It's Sunday and I attend what they call the Sunday school, an activity for children and teenagers during the Sunday service. The man leading the group, an elder in the church who attended the first healing and not knowing what had happened after, invites me to give a testimony of what God did in my life this week. I begin my story, happy to have an opportunity to express my deep faith in the healing to come, even if it is not yet manifest. When I start talking about the visit to the doctor and his appraisal, the leader abruptly interrupts me and begins his Bible teaching.

Nobody in that church will ever raise that subject again with me or any of my family.

Some months later, my leg breaks again spontaneously. I had imprudently carried a young girl on my shoulders during a church youth camp. Her weight was enough to cause the fracture.

Hospital again. Surgery. Fortunately, the doctors can remove some of my broken bone to make my legs equal. From this, to his great relief, my father derives the fantastical interpretation of how my "healing" has manifested, that my leg was strong again and (sup-

*posedly and inaccurately) the part removed was the part affected by
the disease.*

*I buy it fully and many times over the years give testimony of
how God always answers prayers, even if sometimes in ways less
spectacular than expected.*

∼

OBVIOUSLY, my illness and frailty are still here. The bone cancer
that cost me my leg, after another spontaneous fracture, was
found in the unstable area "healed" long ago. I relate this experience from my childhood because it illustrates many of the
dynamics at work to produce the fertile soil in which the toxic
Jesuses grow, or to put it differently, the toxic ways of inter-
preting and relating to Jesus. The toxic Jesuses were particularly present and active in my family, as have you certainly
noticed, and therefore in my life as a child. They need to be
exposed as clearly as possible in order to understand what
they're made of, how harmful they are, and how one can get rid
of them and heal.

To tell that story, I connected often with the twelve-year-old
I was when all those events occurred. I listened to him, little by
little able to relive all the feelings, expectations and pressures
he passed through, and how he coped with them. I became intimate with him. I still am.

It may seem strange for me to characterize that twelve-year-
old as someone other than me. Yet in a sense he was. As this
child, I was faced with such strong emotions and conflicts that I
made a difficult though unconscious choice: to repress a whole
range of what I experienced at that time, in order to keep intact
some parts of my existence that I considered vital. From that
moment on, all that experience and feeling were frozen inside
of me. A large part of my being became alienated from me
while still subsisting in a kind of limbo, hoping obscurely to

888

one day regain the right to exist. This stranger, this inner child, I now desperately needed to meet.

When I learned that the leg remaining unhealed, an impossible conflict arose in my mind and heart between two realms:

- The realm of reality and raw facts showing that this whole stuff of healing wasn't working and that there was a big bug in the way my father and his church were seeing God, Bible, prayer, faith and God's way. The realization could have caused a shock, resulting in a healthy rearrangement in how I saw reality in general, allowing me to grow towards adulthood, autonomy, freedom of thought. But...
- In opposition lurked the worldview and the realm of beliefs that my father and the whole church obviously decided to maintain in spite of the evidence. My father was the adult in charge, the figure of authority, and his way of handling the situation was of paramount importance to the child I was. And obviously, no other adult close and trustworthy enough was in a position to offer another option, to confront the foolishness and toxicity of the whole situation.

The child I was made the only possible choice according to his limited perception: to keep his father's love and approbation at any price. As a result, the child I was had to repress a whole range of feelings and perceptions, and I had to deprive myself of important tools that I would need to grow and face life:

- My intelligence and ability to recognize and interpret raw facts to adapt and develop my perception of reality.
- My disappointment and sadness over not being

healed, feelings not given the least chance to be expressed or even felt, neither in my family nor in the church.

- My anger and feeling of having been cheated, my inability to express defiance against the supposed healer.
- My fear and even terror when realizing, if confusedly, that the adults in charge of me were completely unable to cope in a healthy way with the difficult realities of life, including my disease and handicap.

All of this deprivation happened in an instant, at the precise moment when the twelve-year-old I was heard the doctor say I wasn't healed. In that moment, when the implications of that raw fact appeared to me, I had to meet them with immediate suppression.

From that moment on, a new mission overtook my consciousness: instead of seeing facts and adapting to them, thus gradually changing and maturing, I had to use my intelligence to construe elaborate rationalizations, attempting to reconcile beliefs with the facts contradicting them.

From that moment on, I became numb to sadness or any strong emotions. I became resistant to pain, anger, and fear, unable to cry or even to feel anything except a knot of anxiety, which manifested in my throat when I was overwhelmed by the dangerous (as I perceived them) manifestations of my internal life.

Of course that numbness and hardness had already begun in my early years, as I experienced my parents' repeated rejection of all strong emotion. Any emotions were obviously a threat to their worldview and fragile inner equilibrium. In fact, for them, "negative" emotions signalled the same reality that they were trying to protect themselves and their family from. Such feelings were clearly dangerous and subversive.

One important thing must be said: all of this happened "in the name of Jesus" in the darkened backstage of my family life, where all the frailties, wounds, fears and grief lay hidden. Meanwhile, upstage, everything seemed to be, and was, only about faith in Jesus and keeping the good beliefs. None of the inner turmoil was allowed to appear. In fact, onstage the sets were designed to hide and make inaccessible everything that was happening behind the stage.

And so he came to life and grew—that toxic **Jesus the negator**, who wants us to dismiss our own experience, feelings and intelligence. He lurks backstage, behind all the overzealous claims and praises, the faith-based explanations of events.

In the following years, with all my love, zeal, and intelligence, I would give testimony of how Jesus had finally healed me in an unexpected way, involving the intervention of some skilled doctors. I would argue, later, with my theology teachers, trying to preserve my literal and naive reading of the Bible and avoid the discoveries of science, archeology and philology. As a pastor, I could preach with sincerity, pray for people with trust, lead worship with joy and conviction.

All that sincerity, trust, joy and conviction were honest. But offstage lay all the repressed material, highly toxic, contaminating all efforts at true depth and authenticity. The toxic Jesus. Backstage and unconsciously, I couldn't help knowing that this Jesus demanded repression of feelings, denial of any intelligence needed to face facts, and suppression of anger. The same Jesus whom my father served, sacrificing his own capacities and sensibility. The same Jesus who repaid that service by justifying this whole lie, giving it the appearance of true faith and dedication.

Not a New Jesus

This toxic Jesus is present in Church history, as he still is in the daily life of many churches and religious movements today. My hope is that my own singular story may help to point to larger trends and dynamics at work in both ancient and contemporary history. In the same vein, it may help some to realize how they too are victims of similar abuse and suffering from the same toxic influences.

In Church history, every scientific discovery that seems to contradict religious belief or dogma has been systematically met with defiance and rejection. There are at least two obvious examples: Galileo calling into question the central place of Earth in the universe, and Darwin representing human beings as the product of long evolution rather than the spontaneous creation of God. In both cases science brought evidence, based on facts and observation, that obviously contradicted the prevailing belief system embodied in Church doctrine.

The Church's reaction in both cases was in many ways similar to what happened in my own personal story:

- Intense repression, using the power of the Church to fight and try to silence the bearer of the disturbing discoveries: physical power in the form of house arrest for Galileo, moral and political power in the later fight against Darwin.
- Twisted subversion of intelligence, trying either to prove the facts were false or to show how the entrenched belief system could accommodate them. For example, from the nineteenth century until now, how much energy and intelligence have smart and dedicated Christian scientists of all denominations invested in trying to reconcile evolution with the

myth of creation or to prove the historical existence
of Noah's ark?

In doing this, the Church deprived itself of what would
have been a precious opportunity to evolve and grow its under-
standing of spirituality. It might have been possible, if minds
were more open and free, to hasten the advent of a less archaic
way of considering God and spirituality, a more adult and integrated conception. The Church might have avoided the crisis
it's in now, in which its belief system has been reduced almost
to ruins by the increasingly triumphant rationalism of our time,
seemingly leaving the Church with only two choices. It can
regress into religious fundamentalism and a completely back-
ward-looking view of belief, a purely tribal interpretation of
spirituality. Or, it may face increased difficulty in finding a clear
voice to express anything relevant in today's societies. I'll speak
of that later in this book.

So how might all of this affect us?

First: Anyone who follows a religious or spiritual practice
may benefit from trying to recognize if and where they've
been influenced by this toxic representation of Jesus and his
message. Try to discern how some of our efforts to become
better people—our dedication to God and spiritual growth
and the time we've invested in church activities—are
unknowingly subverted to serve hidden toxic Jesuses. It's
important to recognize how we have been deprived of a
portion of our ability to recognize and live our feelings, and
to consider the facts that appear on our way and process
them intelligently.

Second: The same questioning concerns those who have
left any religious practice in the past, whether disappointed or
hurt by church situations, by inappropriate family education,
or for any other reason. Those experiences very likely left deep
inner wounds and imprints, and possibly we still have inner

work to do to reclaim some part of our ability to fully feel, to see clearly, to think and act accurately.

This book doesn't pretend to be a self-help book outlining the three or twelve steps to resolve all your problems easily. I know too well how this process needs time and, in many cases, the help of a skilled therapist trained in integral psychotherapy and shadow work.

But the journey definitely begins with asking questions, accepting doubts, welcoming and listening to disturbing facts.

Some of those questions could be the following:

- Are there any difficult life situations that you've passed through about which you've built a kind of resignation, an acceptance without a lot of feelings except for maybe a low-level melancholy when you think about them?
- Are there any illnesses or accidents or grief where you've been told that it was God's will and you had to accept it, or maybe even praise God for it, or expect it to be resolved by God's grace in His own time?
- Are there life problems in which you have invested a lot of energy, praying for a solution to emerge and yet finding it impossible to do anything concrete?
- Is it easy for you to feel and to express sadness? When is the last time you cried and what for? Are you comfortable with feeling and expressing anger? Are you sometimes overwhelmed by rage and unable to control your behavior?
- When mistreated in any way, is it easy for you to minimize it, to find excuses for those who mistreated you, to accept it with resignation?
- When you face any kind of problem, are you able to mobilize your skills, intelligence, and experience to

analyze and respond to it quickly and effectively? Or
do you have a tendency to postpone, to wait and see,
to let some situations or illnesses evolve and worsen
before you react?

Any of those behaviors or traits may be symptoms of a toxic
Jesus present in your belief system, perhaps buried in the
depths of your inner world, depriving you subtly or grossly of
part of your birthright: to use your innate capacity to feel and
think, to accurately relate to reality and facts, and finally to
grow and mature in the process.

Bringing more light to your belief system is the beginning
of your discovery of your toxic Jesus. It's a difficult yet beautiful
journey, in which one may learn to get rid of this inner poison
and grow into consciousness and an increasing ability to face
life's challenges courageously.

Let's continue that journey in the next chapters by
confronting other toxic Jesuses.

2

JESUS THE PUNISHER

As I described earlier, during my patient listening to the child I had been, I began to feel the dark burden he had to carry, the tyranny he had to endure. At first I felt sad, sharing his own never-consoled sadness. Behind sadness I found the repressed anger. Finally, behind the anger I discovered the fear and even terror he had felt, having been exposed to such wounded and incompetent adults.

As I understood him more completely, with empathy and compassion, I realized that for years I myself had been repressing him, refusing to listen to him and to consider that frozen part inside of me. The oppressed child in me needed me to focus my attention on him. He needed to trust me enough to know that I wouldn't at some point treat him as I had in the past, following my parents' example by again finding ways to ignore and repress his feelings and his pain.

This trust grew, and so did I. As I began to see more clearly my inner repressed world, I made a new saddening discovery: I could sense that the child in me was weary of living under this heavy burden, was deprived of vital energy, was keen to turn towards death and to embrace the deceiving sirens of afterlife consolations as an excuse to renounce life itself. The feeling mirrored what I had seen my father carry throughout his life: the repressed pain and disappointment with reality, leaving him less and less able to invest hope and life force anywhere other than in the expectation of a future heaven and revelation of Christ on Earth.

In short, in that process of deep listening, another toxic Jesus was unveiled: **Jesus the punisher**, who loves death and suffering and wants sacrifice.

Truly, I had been so prone to sacrifice such important parts of my sensibility, giving away most of the power I needed to grow and face life events adequately; so prone to accepting suffering without reaction, to passively enduring my chronic, handicapped condition; so prone to live a life diminished and deprived of juice, interest and force; so prone, in a word, to self-denial that, indeed, there was a kind of submission to and compromise with death.

Again, "in the name of Jesus."

As part of my patient listening, I sensed something else: the child in me began to open to a new hope and vitality. I was for him that adult he had so cruelly been deprived of. He could feel my love and dedication, and he could begin to listen to me and trust me. The progress of our intimacy allowed him to benefit from all that I had learned since those years: all my necessary doubts and questionings, all my hard work to shape a new way of seeing reality, a freer spirituality, an ability to face life's difficulties with maturity, keeping a connection with all that was happening inside me. And so he could begin to heal and grow.

Our intimacy created a space where he could rest and be loved. He found in me that friendly presence he needed so much. In this space was light and freedom. For him to enjoy this space, the encounter between adult and child had to happen.

And so I became more complete, more integrated. It has been a sweet and loving inner reconciliation. I could reclaim the life force, intelligence and sensibility I had been deprived of for so many years. I began to see mechanisms of sabotage and inner criticism that had long poisoned my life from the inside out. I could begin to confront them and get rid of them.

The toxic Jesus I expose here is the punisher, who advocates suffering and self-sacrifice, encouraging his believers to cultivate a poisonous attachment to deprivation and death, inviting them to suffer alongside him and to sacrifice in many different ways.

This whole issue casts a long shadow. Throughout Christian history you find threads of fascination with suffering and sacrifice, rooted in the suffering and death of Jesus himself. Indeed, Jesus died an infamous and unjust death, and in so doing, expressed all the depth of his love for humanity. His death demonstrated how much he identified with the human condition. His resurrection shows that He didn't die in vain, that His love and message reveal His true nature and present the way to find what he calls the kingdom of God. So we see Jesus victorious over death and the sufferings he had to endure, his teaching and actions fully validated.

Things began to get twisted when some parts of the early Church interpreted Jesus's death as a kind of offering made to an angry god in order to bargain for the salvation of humankind through the sacrifice of an innocent victim. Thus the need for blood and suffering began to overshadow the love of the son of God and his identification with humankind. For many of the faithful, sacrifice and suffering became the source of salvation, rather than Jesus's love, life and message. I'll talk more extensively about this in the last chapters.

This trend never ceased and developed in many ways. You can see it in the overvaluing of martyrdom since the first century. In this vein, Christian monks began to abuse their bodies, using various forms of self-punishment in order to attain higher levels of spirituality. Irish monks in the sixth century, for example, often prayed for hours immersed up to their hips in the glacial water of the Irish Sea, hoping to strengthen their souls by mortifying their bodies. You see it later in the morbid and almost pornographic fascination of some painters with the wounds and tortured body of Jesus in images of the crucifixion, for example, in German and Spanish late gothic art.

In contemporary Catholic movements, a practice still exists that has been common especially in some monastic orders and clergy over the centuries: the practice of "discipline," repeatedly beating one's own back with a whip made of nine knotted ropes, with the goal of participating in Christ's suffering and obtaining its spiritual benefits. Pope Jean-Paul II himself, among many others, was reportedly practicing discipline in his private devotion, without publicly recommending it to the faithful.

The practice is less prevalent in evangelical or protestant circles, but the morbid fascination with suffering still appears, especially in the persistent theme of sacrifice as atonement demanded by an angry God, as well as in the rituals and teachings focused on the blood of Christ. I find something scary and somewhat schizophrenic in this image of God, the father, loving humanity to the point that he sent his "only son" to die horrifically, yet who is at the same time so angry and demanding that he needs even more sacrifice.

Most of us, hopefully, aren't submitting ourselves to such extreme practices as using a whip to better commune with Jesus. Nonetheless, the preoccupation with death, suffering and sacrifice exists within us in different forms. It's generated when twisted comprehensions and representations of Jesus meet with unresolved and unconscious inner wounds and suffering, resulting in the belief in a toxic Jesus, poisoning the depths of our being.

How can you recognize whether some of your devotion and love are unknowingly misdirected in serving this toxic Jesus, the punisher? It may concern you not only if you practice any kind of religion or spirituality, but also if you have been exposed to this influence through your education, your culture, or your parents' beliefs.

For me I might have been alerted by an early symptom: as a teenager I couldn't help discreetly crying when seeing any representation of the crucifixion in a movie. The problem is, it was the *only* time as a teenager when tears came to my eyes. Otherwise, I had learned to endure pain and anxiety during my repeated stays in hospitals, following my parents' example of systematically ignoring or repressing strong emotions.

One of my earlier childhood memories involves my crying all the tears in my body, inconsolable after hearing the story of a mother pelican sacrificing herself by pecking out her belly to feed her babies. I now think this was a natural reaction, expressing the realization of a young child that his own mother's life was subsumed by taking care of others, projecting her own needs onto what she imagines them wanting or needing, no matter what their real wants and needs were.

Some might feel touched by my former sensibility to sacrifice and presume it was a kind of expression of love for Jesus. But now I clearly see how it was really the expression of an unhealthy, hidden leaning towards death and sacrifice. I was unconsciously convinced that I too had to sacrifice myself. I was following that double example of Jesus and my mother and obeying my father's fundamentalist injunctions.

Here again—a toxic Jesus!

It's useful to notice that, while being so sensitive to images of Jesus dying on the cross, I was on the other hand almost completely numb to any emotion related to my own life. I hid that emotional void behind a strong appearance of dedication and availability to others, and a constant smile even when I should have been angry, disappointed or desperate. This behavior was more or less satisfactory for my public life as a pastor, but totally inappropriate for intimacy, including with my own inner life.

It took years of therapy, meditation, and facing life's struggles to gradually reclaim a true connection with my emotions and to lose that façade. More and more could I connect with my inner desires, needs and impulses, become more intimate with my own emotions, and so reclaim power over my own life.

But it's only recently that I could see clearly how that compulsion to self-sacrifice was associated with a twisted image of Jesus and how, despite all the inner work I had already done, the tendency to tolerate and submit passively to suffering remained within me, clogging my soul. It has been a true liberation, resulting in a renewed desire to live and a stronger consciousness of the value—and at the same time the fragility —of each instant. Death is not negated, but it is no longer confusedly associated with the longing for a fantasy afterlife or overlife (full of angels, demons, glories and terrors). Death takes its due place, always present and reminding me that life is finite, thus giving full value to every moment and experience.

As I said, the toxic Jesus who loves death and suffering and demands sacrifice lies in a dark shadow of Christianity. If you have been raised in a Christian family, it's highly possible that you have been exposed to that twisted spirituality. Depending on your own wounds and hidden pains, you may have embraced part of it deeply, resulting in poisonous fruits inside your inner life.

Track it without mercy. Expose it. Rebuke it. Claim your birthright to live, to heal, to feel, to be free, to grow.

This work, though it may be long and painful, is very much

worth doing. It allows energy to flow through your inner life and outer experiences, resulting in a sense of vitality and freedom so precious and exhilarating. You deserve nothing less.

In the next chapter, I'll expose the toxic Jesus who is most closely related to this one.

3

JESUS THE MAGICIAN

L ife is hard. Shit happens—more than once in a lifetime. And most of the time we have good reason to feel overwhelmed when we face dramatic challenges such as serious illness, the death of someone we love, a natural or political event that threatens our existence.

Both my father and mother, as very young children, had to face war. As a consequence, my father endured the tragic separation of his parents and his mother's struggle to survive and find food and subsistence. My mother had to face her father's unemployment and the subsequent necessity for the family to move fourteen times in five years from country to country in a never-ending quest for a lasting job and security.

How did those children feel, seeing their parents desperately trying to find ways of facing those events? Seeing them full of fear, sadness, doubts and worries about the future and the present? Seeing them doing their best but never sure whether they could overcome the obstacles, whether they can even survive? Seeing adversity and threats all around them and their families?

How affected these children must have been seeing the

relative helplessness of their parents in these difficult situations. As a child, you need to see your father and mother as the ones in charge, the strong ones who know what to do, those who are able to help you with any problem you face. You rely on them for all your basic needs. Your survival is in their hands. How terrifying is it to perceive, even on an unconscious level, that they're not in charge of everything, their power is limited as they face problems bigger than them, remaining uncertain even with their best efforts.

Certainly that's what my parents faced in their early childhood. It's nearly impossible for a child this age to cope with the feelings that arise when he or she sees parents overwhelmed. Such feelings are so threatening that they are often repressed and even buried deep inside one's body.

Repressed trauma produces devastating effects on one's future development, at least when it remains untreated and hidden behind strong barriers. In my father's case, the result was a constant melancholy and fear of life, which he tried to mitigate with moral rigidity and repressed rage that often surfaced behind his severe and controlled facade. My mother numbed herself to any feeling and tried to cope with life's difficulties and her own pervasive anxiety by taking care of others and oversimplifying reality, inhabited by the conviction that she could face anything and knew others' needs and how to fulfill them better than they did.

The debilitating effects of trauma are not limited to those who have suffered firsthand: the stress can pass through generations in unconscious but nonetheless toxic ways. Indeed, epigenetic expressions have been observed in children and grandchildren of holocaust survivors. More obvious is the influence of education and example provided by traumatized parents who share with their children not only what they decide but everything they are: best and worst, hidden and manifest.

Where unresolved trauma meets religion lies fertile ground for another toxic Jesus—the Magician, who expects things to come from above and wants us to do the same.

Of course religion may be a source of authentic comfort. The belief in a loving power at work behind life events may be reassuring and help mobilize one's own resources for coping and holding out hope. But when religion covers hidden trauma, a different kind of belief and attitude towards life may emerge. For example, in order to face the terror of the inner child who has seen one's parents overwhelmed by life events, one can be tempted to adhere to a simplistic vision: that a higher power controls everything and can intervene miraculously in any situation.

Why is such a belief toxic? Let me go back to the example described earlier: when confronted with my genetic disease, my father first remained totally passive, almost absent, not talking with me about it, hardly even visiting me during the months I spent in the hospital. He told me later that he had spent hours praying hard for me so that I could heal and be able to cope with the situation. This came as no surprise to me, but his actions were confined to prayer alone. When the promise of a miracle appeared in the person of the healer invited in our church, he naturally thought it was God's answer to his prayers.

Facing this difficult situation, my father took refuge in his belief in a God that was in control and was able to change everything. He renounced his power to face it, since it would necessarily have been imperfect and limited. His faith provided him with a deceptive refuge for his own terrified internal child, but left him impotent to address the real issues facing his family.

Adherents to this belief perceive Jesus as the supreme example of the same attitude: he is seen as passive and totally submissive to his father in heaven, all powerful and totally in control. When Jesus performs a miracle, the miracle is an answer to his prayers and faith. Jesus is so powerful because he submits to God's will. When faced with the prospect of his death on the cross, he simply accepts it without complaint.

Derived from this interpretation of Jesus's good works and final surrender comes the construct that the attitude of the true believer towards life and life's challenges must be in submitting to God's will. From obedience and faith comes the possibility of benefitting from God's power from above and soothing our suffering or giving it meaning by making it part of his plan. Faith becomes almost synonymous with passivity and resignation; the only activity of any real use is prayer.

This toxic Jesus has two sides, the miracle side and the fatalistic side.

- On the miracle side lies the hope that in even the worst situation, something miraculous can happen and God can change it for the best. He can even stop the sun from moving, if it helps His armies win a holy battle. Of course, the possibility of a miracle depends on the faith of the believers.

- On the fatalistic side lies the conviction that even adverse circumstances are a direct expression of God's will towards us. Indeed, some bestsellers in Christian circles advocate that the true believer must give thanks to God and rejoice with faith for everything that happens to him, even the most traumatic events. God being love, everything expresses his love and so must be met with praise.

On both sides lie a *terror and rejection of reality*.

Both sides of this Jesus registered as deep belief for me. Belief in a Jesus that could do miracles for me if I would believe enough. Belief in an all-powerful God that was in control of every event of my life, with a clear intent for me that I had to understand in order to follow his orders.

But most of all was the belief that behind the surface of reality lay an unbearable and all pervasive terror that I needed to avoid at any price.

How often have I seen my father trying to escape this terror by elaborating increasingly sophisticated and obsessive belief systems, while his only real intent was to push this terror away and to find some relief from its constant oppression:

- Belief either in the future of a fascinating and terrible apocalypse, with all the motifs that inhabited his fears: war, demons, torture and persecution, famine, natural catastrophes, and the intervention of the all-powerful Jesus with legions of angels to oppose the forces of evil.
- Belief in the upper- or underworld of the spiritual war happening right now behind the veil (or reality), full of battles, angels, demons, the devil himself and, above all, Jesus as the warlord for God, controlling the situation.

This Jesus is so toxic because he promotes a completely immature and ineffective way to integrate reality and face the difficult discovery that we are not at the center of a secure world. And in doing that, he deprives his believers of a crucial part of their humanity. As humans, most of us have been given many intellectual and physical tools that are needed to face life's difficulties in effective ways. When we use these tools, we are more likely to endure or overcome difficulties, as our ancestors have in the face of many threats. Through our intelligence, intuition, sensibility and strength, we create, collaborate, plan and build. We develop institutions, structures, techniques. As a species, at least until now, we survive and grow. As individuals, we have resources to help us face much of what happens to us. We can't face everything, but we can face a lot.

Let me give you a personal example from recent experience. Three months after my leg amputation I had an important appointment for a scan and an MRI to check whether my body was still free of cancer. As you can imagine, the state of expectation and tension during the many days before was intense. On the appointed day I called the hospital with a question in the morning, and to my surprise I learned that the tests had been cancelled. After some research, it appeared that an assistant had made a mistake. Everybody was very sorry and promised that the appointment secretary would do her best to find a new date, hopefully the week after, but no guarantee ("it's very difficult, you know...")—despite my insistence that they find a quicker solution. After the call, I began to resign myself to more days of anxiety. Then I was suddenly struck by a righteous anger: I don't deserve to be treated like this; I am not going to endure this passively! I called the doctor directly and then his secretary, demanding a solution and proposing they send me to a private clinic equipped with the adequate machines. To my surprise, they organized that solution in ten minutes for the day after.

In my former "believer's" way of facing things, inherited from my parents, I would probably have prayed that the secretary would find a quicker solution. I would have abandoned the situation to God's hands, telling him how much I was trusting him, waiting for him to intervene. When confronted with the likely issue that the exam would happen two weeks later, I would have repressed my disappointment and taken that as an opportunity to build my faith and to endure anxiety with more courage. And I would have suffered silently. Even years later, when I wasn't thinking and believing that way anymore, the influence of this toxic Jesus was expressed in a strong tendency towards passivity and resignation.

But having resolutely confronted that toxic Jesus through my therapeutic work and my life experience, I was able to mobilize my limited resources to face the situation. I used my relational skills to explain to the doctor and convince him that the situation wasn't tolerable. I put a bit of pressure on the secretary. I used my intelligence to think of an adequately equipped private clinic and then I proposed it. There was no guarantee of success. I hadn't much power, actually, but I used it. It could have turned out otherwise. (By the way, the test results were good, no trace of cancer, which was a big relief.)

To spot the traces of this toxic Jesus's influence in one's life, some of the following questions and considerations may help you:

- What is the importance of any kind of overlife or afterlife belief in terms of your coping with reality?
- To be more specific: do you have strong expectations of miraculous solutions to your problems coming from outside yourself, be it from God, from the universe, from synchronicity, from the law of attraction?
- Do you believe strongly in life after death, in the kingdom of God coming to earth in the future, in any kind of apocalypse?
- To put it more softly, do you have daydreams or fantasies that you cultivate to help you bear situations that you shouldn't have to bear, to endure mistreatment, to submit passively to illness or to any kind of suffering?

Not that those beliefs or expectations are all wrong. But do they help you cope with any unpleasant reality in a way that prevents you from taking the steps necessary to deal with it or putting healthy boundaries in place and changing what can be changed?

Any of those beliefs and behaviors could point to a hidden devotion to this toxic Jesus. The good news is that freedom begins with consciousness, and that you're doing the work, perhaps in this precise moment of reading, to bring those shadows into the light. Anything that deprives you of your ability to use your skills fully and to seize opportunities to face life's challenges must be attributed to a toxic and hidden belief from which you can be freed. Anything that drives you into resignation, fatalism or passive acceptance, though it be clothed in the most beautiful spiritual explanations, must be swept into the dustbin.

Instead, let consciousness penetrate through those depths to a place where a fearful child may need to be met. Dare to become intimate with those fears, terrors, feelings of helplessness, and sadness that you froze when they became unbearable. Be that adult that can now bear them, take that child under your protection and teach him/her that life may be lived —and remain worthy of it, even through all the difficulties that may arise.

And live!

And face things that happen the best you can!

If necessary, find a skilled, solidly trained therapist and begin the journey to more integration, joy and freedom.

4

JESUS THE OPPRESSOR

I n the last three chapters, I described in detail the central dynamics that make the bed for so many toxic beliefs and therefore give birth to three of the toxic Jesuses.

There are many more. Their immense capacity for adaptation and camouflage allows them to sneak in everywhere one tries to bypass any kind of fear, suffering or traumatic memory, using and twisting religious beliefs and spirituality.

And of course, as human beings, because we share many of the same wounds and frailties, it's no wonder that many of those toxic Jesuses have manifested collectively, showing up and pouring their poison throughout Christian history and indeed the history of all other religions and spiritual beliefs— in different forms and by other names, but nonetheless harming people and depriving them of their human dignity in the same way.

Anybody becoming familiar with their own zone of shadows, and with the toxic beliefs that hide in them, is going to discover their own tribe of toxic Jesuses and will have to know them well to get rid of their influence.

The following chapters are about some more toxic Jesuses I found in my own experience and who needed to be exposed.

To face them, I went on opening the doors of my inner world, and I let the memories come to me. I discovered that the toxic Jesuses were hidden in plain sight. I didn't have to go looking for repressed or inaccessible memories. The child, the adolescent, the young adult that I was took care to engrave these key moments in my memory. Nothing was hidden from me. Everything was there, I just didn't have eyes to see it. It took the liberating shock of reality for the blinders to fall and these memories to deliver their messages.

In the next three chapters, I will describe three memories that condense and reveal the presence of these other toxic Jesuses that I have unmasked in me. These memories were gateways to my awareness and healing, and I feel eternally grateful to that part of me that, by remembering, acted as guardian of my wound and therefore retained the echo of unease and oppression over the years.

Here is the first of these memories:

Teenage years again, between twelve and fourteen. We are seated as a family; the midday meal is coming to an end. My father speaks with conviction about several people, colleagues or members of the church. He analyzes, criticizes, judges. Severe, he explains to my mother how they should act differently, be different ...

My father has said it many times: he thinks he has the "gift of discernment," a supernatural ability given by the Holy Spirit that allows him to counsel people and see clearly what must change in their lives. With a lump in my throat, I join the discussion and try to put into words what I vaguely perceive: "Why are you talking about all these people in our presence? It doesn't concern us, my sister and me. And you're just criticizing them... Is that what you call your famous gift of discernment?"

I don't remember the argument that ensued. Just my father's face, red with repressed anger. And I see myself a few hours later in my room, upset, wracked with fear and guilt, frantically reading my bible, highlighting a passage and scribbling a few words in the margin... I found this bible not long ago, and I came across the passage that I had underlined: "Children, obey your parents in all things, for this is pleasant in the Lord," and my own words in pencil, in my adolescent handwriting: "I must not destroy my father's ministry by opposing him!"

How clearly the toxic Jesuses show up in this memory! And how deeply had I already internalized them! How spontaneously they manifested themselves in my tormented consciousness, to the point of suppressing in me any hint of revolt, any criticism of the system of oppression under which we were all living, my father, my mother, my sister and me!

Jesus the castrator, who makes humans small and disempowered; **Jesus the oppressor**, who gives power to tyrants; **Jesus the patriarchalist**, who requires submission to the established order, and therefore to the Father and to his undivided domination—they all act together to keep their subjects in terror.

Their first victim, in this situation, was my father. He was full of doubts about himself. He lived with the constant feeling of his inadequacy and unworthiness. It took me a long time to understand it, and to open myself to compassion for him. His wound fascinated and terrified him. He could not discover the injured child who was hiding in it—this terrorized child he had been, abandoned, hoping for the help and comfort of a benevolent adult. But listening to the wound, opening up, was unthinkable to him. The adult was too helpless, the child seemed too hurt. The vulnerability seemed too threatening.

And so, in the absence of this openness, the wound became the breach through which **Jesus the castrator** could enter, with the fallacious promise of relieving the helplessness and worthlessness. This is how my father became trapped. Trapped by a god who supposedly wanted him weak and helpless, like a beggar, in constant need of an external power to compensate for his fragility.

Contempt for the human, fascination with and idealization of what can only come from above. Submission. Jesus the castrator also becomes **Jesus the oppressor**, who first subjected my father to his tyranny, then through my father, exercised this tyranny over those around him, first of all over his family. Submission is the price of solace for perceived unworthiness, and even more for trying to deny the fragility of existence.

This is how the castrator and the oppressor establish the reign of **Jesus the patriarchalist**. He is the guarantor of this system of domination. Human beings, men and women, cannot exist in their own power, for there must be no other power than that from above, that of the fantasized Supreme Father. The relationship of domination becomes the basis of all relationships: domination of the Father over Jesus, the totally submissive son and therefore repository of power from above, then all other dominions, that of the human by the divine, woman by man, child by adult, nature by the human race, etc.

What about me? No choice, I thought. I followed in my father's footsteps. I denied my feelings, my own revolt, and at the same time my own power, and so I tried to keep my father intact. I stifled my revolt against his claims, and yet I could see that there was a form of tyranny behind his "famous gift," something unjust, something against which it would have been healthy to rebel.

This attitude is emblematic of what toxic spirituality produces: as I learned to suppress my emotions, my intelligence, my intuition, I also had to bend under the yoke and learn to stifle any legitimate revolt. I learned to ignore or underestimate the impact of the domination relationships that I saw around me, and even more, of those that I was victim of. And of course, this opened the door for me, in turn, to become perpetrator of this tyranny towards others.

How enriched I have been in reconnecting with this angry teenager. How rich was his suppressed revolt. I found in this part of me a vital energy that I did not even suspect. And with it came resources of wisdom and discernment. This teenager was sensitive to injustice, he was full of hope and courage to face it, he was creative and intelligent enough to imagine paths of repair and change. But he needed an adult to validate his feelings, to help him channel his energy, to reassure him and love him. An adult who was at peace with his own fragility as a human being, and at the same time aware of his strengths and resources.

This adult was not there forty years ago. There was only the fragility of his father, that of his mother, and his own. The teenager therefore decided to submit. But today, the adult I am can welcome, love and accompany this teenager who is still there deep inside me. And so, I regain possession of this buried part of my virile strength. It is a part of my dignity as a human being. At the same time, I make peace with my own fragility. Anger, energy, discernment, wisdom, resources, courage, freedom, creativity and healthy humility are returned to me. And I enjoy my ability to create equal and healthy relationships with my human sisters and brothers as with myself, born from this strength, this conscience and this dignity.

And to my surprise, I also find in myself a tenderness and compassion for my father and my mother, once I have faced revolt, anger and sadness. I see the wound and the child in both of them. And perhaps I can welcome this wound and these children more than they could, beyond time and death.

Too often in their history, Christian churches have fallen into this trap set for each religion. They too found themselves part of this relationship of domination: being both victims and perpetrators at the same time, failing to welcome the human beings confronted with their frailty and their wounds.

Too often, that's how Christians of all times have been asked to abdicate their own ability to face things in favor of submission to a superior power. Trapped in such a system of coping with reality, they come to defy their own selves more and more. The whole range of human experience, abilities, sensibility, intuition, intelligence looks corrupted by what they have learned to call sin.

That's how Jesus the castrator gathers a flock of eunuchs, men and women deeply defiant of everything they are and full of fears and inhibitions. They always have to wonder if what they do is flawed by their innately sinful nature, and are therefore prone to guilt and passivity. What is amputated from them is their ability as human beings to face life's challenges actively and with dignity.

How many people have I seen like that in churches? They are trying to be "good Christians," but are always in doubt, chronically subjected to guilt. They repress their anger. They deny their deepest and best impulses and feelings. They are anxious to discern "God's will" before daring to take any significant action.

God is big!

God knows!

God is powerful!

God must be adored!

This god is so big that he takes all the space. There is no space left for human beings. Even to consider using human resources, human skills, and human power seems to deprive this big god of some of what belongs to him.

As a teenager and young adult, I only wanted god to become greater and myself to become less. My own person was an embarrassment, an obstacle for the manifestation of god's greatness.

Depriving women and men of their power, this toxic Jesus gives power to the tyrants who strive to establish their rule over people. He becomes the corner stone of patriarchalism and of every system of domination.

As I've said, faith can be and is for many a great resource for facing life. It can provide a true sense of confidence, built on the conviction of being unconditionally loved and welcomed by God. Sin as well can be a helpful concept if it helps people identify a tendency toward self-delusion, toward mistaking projections and illusions for realities.

But too often, Christianity has wandered far away from that safe place, shaming women and men for their bodies, their emotions, their desires, and teaching them to guard against their intelligence and impulses. In different ways throughout history, rather than recognizing and soothing wounds and offering compassion, Christian churches have painted pictures of toxic Jesuses on their walls, in attempts to establish their domination.

You can see examples of this in the many depictions of Christ in majesty in big cathedrals, where Jesus severely watches the flock gathered under his eyes while holding a globe, symbol of his pervasive power over humanity. He sits on the same throne, in the same position and with the same clothes as the human emperors of those times. Of course these works of arts can be faith-inspiring. But so often they have been created to express and justify the political power of emperors and kings, not to mention the prelates who commissioned the works. Much too often, these imaginative visions of power reflected and reinforced real tyrannic oppression.

That oppression extends today to anyone subjected to toxic Jesuses. Already deprived of so much of our resources, we become defenseless against external and internal tyrants. This toxic faith gives them power over us, or more accurately, makes us helplessly accept their usurpation of our own power.

Outwardly, the tyrant can be a parent, a priest, a pastor, a boss, a political leader, anybody who, at a given moment, has power over us and begins to exert it in an abusive way. The internal tyrant is our inner critic, the little voice that relays to us the influence of the external tyrants, grossly or subtly criticizing us in the background of our minds, shaming us, pointing the finger at our faults.

This oppression does not only manifest at the individual level. Jesus the castrator, Jesus the oppressor and Jesus the patriarchalist join hands to justify and maintain every form of repressive and tyrannical social structure: racism, injustice, homophobia, and all kinds of domination and rejection of the other.

I reflected on this aspect of collective repression to try to discern this influence of the toxic Jesus around me. It makes me feel the smell of Mado's coffee and see the kindness and benevolence the tyranny tried to hide under to maintain its grip:

I am in the early years of my ministry as a pastor. Every Tuesday morning, our pastoral team meets at Mado's for what we call the weekly briefing. Mado is a charming lady, single and close to retirement, who has a soft voice. In the parish, she is responsible for visiting the elderly and the sick. She also organizes Sunday school and works with children during Sunday service. For more than 20 years, she was a missionary in West Africa. Upon her return, our parish hired her to assist Gerald, the main pastor, and save her from the financial misery that awaits elderly missionaries returning home. This occurred a few years before I joined to take charge of the youth.

Mado loves coffee, and she welcomes us every week in her tiny, pretty living room. Around a steaming coffee maker and cookies, we discuss not only the life of the parish but also different subjects depending on our concerns and mood. These are warm, friendly, and respectful moments. We always strive to find harmony in the projects we develop and in the opinions we share. I appreciate these two people. They are much older than I am, and their experience and kindness inspire me. They give me security in the apprenticeship of my ministry.

Mado gently teases me about Africa each time we discuss it. I had recently traveled to West Africa myself for a study trip. My wife and I wanted to find out whether or not the life of a missionary called to us. We joined a team of young people and visited several missionaries in Burkina Faso and Niger.

I came back with two strong impressions. The first is that my wife and I definitely feel called to Geneva. Thank God! I now think that this conviction expresses above all our confused, but lucid, perception that we are too hurt, and our balance too precarious, for the dangers and difficulties of such a commitment. My second impression is the great respect I feel for several African pastors we met during the trip. Their intelligence and resources impressed me as they met the challenges posed to them by their economic and social conditions.

When I talk about it, I face Mado's skeptical and amused pout. My naivety moves her, she who knows Africa and Africans so well. She likes to tell us about her memories from the mission, which always demonstrate the necessary influence of the white man and missionary to lead and supervise the "blacks." The "blacks" are inclined to return to their idolatrous practices or dissolute morals if left to fend for themselves. Our parish is committed to financially supporting several missionaries in Africa and elsewhere.

Another topic that regularly raises tensions is inner wounds and psychological help. Gerald and Mado express their reluctance to consider these points. I speak to them regularly about pastors and books that propose a Christianized form of psychological counseling, an aspect of pastoral work I am sensitive to and practice. However, they are wary of too much psychology. The sufferings of the human soul are to be treated mainly with prayer, benevolent listening, and the prescription of passages from the Scriptures to meditate on and submit to. *Everyone has to take charge and exercise their will to adopt behaviors in accordance with biblical standards. This principle applies particularly to issues of a sexual nature, particularly homosexuality.*

However, we do not allow these small tensions and disagreements to disturb our pleasant communion. We return very quickly to less controversial matters. I tell myself that they are from another generation, that it is normal, that mentalities will change slowly, and that I will manage gradually to convince them.

I do not realize the extent to which we share the same conception of the world, even even if our understandings differ in terms of certain nuances. This conception is rooted in violence and arrogance, expressed by the need to change others' beliefs and lives to be more like us. This is the case for mission. This is the case for homosexuality. I speak of welcoming homosexual people into the church, but this is to "heal" their condition and reconcile them not only with God but also with their masculinity or femininity, according to their gender.

I am blind to the violence, arrogance, and pretension that hide behind the so-called kindness and good intentions of our group. It is only much later that I began to realize our parish was remarkably homogeneous: composed almost exclusively of white, lower-middle class, Swiss people who are poorly educated, well integrated into society, and apparently heterosexual.

Many years after leaving this milieu and the Evangelical faith, a member of the group of young people I had led named Adrian resumes contact with me. We had been close for many of my pastoral years before losing touch when he went to study in the United States.

Listening to him, I discover with shame and sadness the suffering and oppression he went through during those years in the parish. As a young teenager, he began to realize his homosexuality, but there was no room for that in our community. No room to talk about it. No room to think about it, even. It couldn't exist. His path to accepting himself and learning to love himself was long and painful. My colleagues and I have been, with all of our kindness and benevolence, instruments in the hands of the poisonous Jesus, and contributed to the oppression and rejection he suffered.

Today, Adrian leads an inclusive movement within the Protestant Church for LGBTIQ+ people of all origins, beliefs, and religions. I am very grateful that he has returned to me and that we have become friends.

5

JESUS THE PURITAN

This internalized tyranny of course affected my relationship with my own sexuality, with women and with my body.

The following memory encapsulates this tyranny:

I am thirteen, in the middle of high school. The hormones are boiling inside me, but I don't know what to do with this storm. I am fascinated by masturbation, but terrified at the same time. I associate it with the first step towards Hell, the threshold that should not be crossed. I strive to stay strong and pure, and so far, I have achieved it. (It won't last!)

The same goes for the girls in my class: they attract me with an intensity that possesses me. I think of them all the time, and yet "dating" one of them is inconceivable. It's difficult because the storm is not only raging within me: all my classmates are actively engaged in the discovery of what "dating" means. I have already had to explain that it wouldn't be possible for me because I'm a Christian.

I remember three of these girls who were intrigued by my attitude. One day, taking advantage of a quieter moment during geography class, they approach me and sit around my desk. They pose an ultimatum: *"Why don't you want to go out with a girl? Choose one of the three of us." I find them so pretty, their proposal is so attractive, and yet I remember with sadness my preemptive inner judgment on them: "They are whores."*

Determined to honor my Christian commitment, I answer them with confidence: "Wait until the end of the day, and I will explain why I don't want to date one of you." My plan is as follows: in the bible, I recently read a passage that says that if a Christian is faced with those who persecute him, the Holy Spirit himself will put in his mouth the words to answer them: "Open your mouth, and I will fill it, saith the Lord." I fantasize that I am this Christian martyr in front of a court.

I hope to kill two birds with one stone: living this experience of the Holy Spirit who puts his words in my mouth seems supremely interesting to me. And at the same time, I'll "bear witness" to my faith to these three girls, because during this same period, I am tormented by the awareness of my responsibility as a Christian: I must speak of Jesus to those around me. All these classmates do not know him, so they are not "saved;" they will go to Hell after their death, and I will be partly responsible for it if I do not "testify." So I spend the rest of the day praying inwardly, asking God to fill my mouth with his words when I face these three girls.

The fateful moment arrives: the last class ends, and they are waiting for me as I leave school. I walk over to them, try to speak. I open my mouth, but nothing comes out. Absolutely nothing. I see myself, mouth wide open, in front of my three comrades, taken aback. In desperation, I try to "prime the pump" and say the first words that come to my mind: "As a good Christian..." and I wait ... and nothing. I do not remember the reaction of these three girls. Maybe they laughed. I know I ran away, filled with shame and confusion. So I was unworthy of divine help.

My heart is tight as I invoke this memory. I see this teenager and all the poison that he has already swallowed, tortured in his relationship with himself and with others. I see his loneliness. Yet I also see a bit of his sincere impulse towards mystery, his true attraction to the divine, hidden behind all the stereotypes and fanatical tendencies.

This teenager was the product of oppression and patriarchalism. My relationship to my body, my sexuality, my masculinity and my femininity were the first victims, killing the possibility of a healthy, free, joyful relationship with myself, with others and with the opposite sex.

I thus discover my submission to another toxic Jesus: **Jesus the misogynist,** who hates and oppresses women.

One constant expression of tyranny is the oppression of women. If you consider how the historic Jesus treated women with respect and consideration, giving them a place among his supporters and even among his nearest disciples and apostles, it seems unlikely that Christianity could become historically such a patriarchal and misogynist religion.

Yet it has been. From the beginning the early Church seems to have been uncomfortable specifically with that aspect of their master's behavior—at least some currents of opinion among the multiplicity of groups with different beliefs and sensibilities who claimed faith in Jesus. Unfortunately, precisely those currents are the ones that prevailed over time, and this is how we conceive of the early Church.

The winners write the history, and consequently nothing remains but indirect traces of the place that women occupied in many of those early movements. One positive trace is the beautiful figure of Mary Magdalene, which the official gospels didn't dare to totally erase, who was sent by Jesus as the first apostle to witness his resurrection and announce it to the other disciples.

Most other traces are hidden under injunctions, spread throughout the New Testament, that try to minimize the role women occupied in early Christian groups: forbidding them to teach (which only confirms they were indeed doing so in many places), relegating them to their traditional roles as wives and mothers (which means that at least some of them were occupying important functions to the point of threatening male leadership), enjoining them to submission and silence.

And sadly, those very texts became the building blocks of women's subsequent and enduring oppression and relegation throughout Christian history.

This again in the name of Jesus, creating yet another oppressive toxic version of him.

As with the submission to tyrants, this oppression of women became internalized by those enduring it. Women too often even endorse the shaming they are submitted to, and so disempower themselves, hiding their precious qualities and skills. Men endorse the patriarchal and oppressive teachings and learn along the way to repress their own femininity. Thus the sexes become antagonistic, deprived at some level of their complementarity and mutual support.

This antagonism leads to the inability to relate in a healthy way to one's own body and sexuality, which is why Jesus the misogynist is also **Jesus the pure spirit**, disincarnate and antisexual.

In the hardworking existence devoid of pleasure, where one always remains frustrated by the never-ending pursuit of a higher goal, the body has a hard time: it's nothing more than a vehicle, a tool, an object. One has to use it in order to attain goals, but in no case do we have to listen to it, to be aware of its fatigue, to respect its signals of distress. The body is just a machine that needs to be fed and grudgingly given some rest, to be taken care of minimally and only in order to do its job.

In Church teachings generally, there is a clear dichotomy between heaven and earth, spiritual and material, spirit and flesh. This toxic Jesus promotes a spirituality that is all about detaching from the body and the material world, supposedly in order to better reach the spiritual realm, where everything good and valuable resides exclusively. It follows that sexuality must be repressed and seen as antithetical to spirituality.

This toxic Jesus presents himself as the ultimate example of the domination of the mind and spirit over the body. His incarnation was an unpleasant necessity, to show us how to follow this path and master our bodies like him, and so become free from our own incarnation. After his death and resurrection, he returned to his higher spiritual state, freed at least from this burden of matter. Truly, in this worldview, matter and the material realm are "what's the matter."

In various ways this contempt for the body and repression of sexuality have been constant trends throughout Church history, most of the time encouraging believers to relate in defiant and utilitarian ways to their bodies. This seems surprisingly contradictory given the doctrine of incarnation, so important in Christian theology, which insists on the belief that God decided to become human, to present Himself in our world as the body of Jesus. This belief could have offered the wonderful opportunity of developing a positive perspective on our bodily existence, but that has rarely been the case throughout centuries of Christian theology.

And that led to the creation of **Jesus the Puritan,** who despises human experience and pleasure.

It's so important for happiness and balance in life to be able to treat yourself kindly, and to do the same for others. It's precious to be able to enjoy and share simple moments, good food, rest, tenderness and friendship. While daily human experience may often be difficult, precarious and exposed to suffering, it is also made up of many little and big pleasures. For those open to seeing them, there are so many occasions for marveling. Even the mere fact of breathing, so simple and unconscious, can be a source of pure joy, as many people who meditate can attest.

The Puritan Jesus has a very different point of view. He

despises openness and kindness, and refuses his adepts as much pleasure as possible. Suspicion and contempt best describe what they must feel towards their own human experience. Pleasure, rest, satisfaction are all suspect: you better be busy improving your spiritual life, working harder for the realization of God's plan, fighting against inner and outer enemies. Life must be a constant battlefield, a place of struggle to reach a higher goal, a more spiritual state, a holier life, a sharper authenticity.

I don't mean to suggest that growth, maturation and learning aren't sometimes best achieved in difficult and radical ways. But to truly take root in our lives, those achievements need to happen in an environment of trust, openness and inner rest. Rest is actually the perfect condition for grace. And rest takes place when we learn to be kind towards ourselves, to treat ourselves well, and to receive with gratitude the precious life we've been given, moment by moment. Of course we have struggles, suffering and longings, but it's possible to learn to make space for them in that place of peace and rest, and it changes the way we relate to them.

From the demands of the toxic Jesus, there is no place for rest, for pleasure or for grace. Only haste and ever-frustrated longing. Only hardworking, severe and sad warriors, wounded and tired.

I was already one of them at thirteen. Misogynist, cut off from myself, puritan, I repressed the vital impulse that invited me to open up to my body, my sexuality, my enjoyment, the discovery of the other sex, relationships. I replaced that with fear, contempt, harshness and fanaticism, following in the footsteps of centuries of submission to these poisonous Jesuses.

These poisons were so deeply embedded in me that it took time and violent shocks for me to see the extent of their influence and get rid of them, even long after I had turned my back on my evangelical faith. It took me a long time to learn to treat myself well, and therefore to treat my body well. I had to go through the shock of divorce and the collapse of the very foundations of my existence. I had to discover the love, joy and pleasure that can be shared in a relationship of respect and partnership. Finally, I had to suffer the shock of illness, which called me to a renewed relationship with my body.

6

JESUS THE FANATIC

I n this last memory, I don't remember my age well. Maybe two or three years after the previous memory. In it appear the last three toxic Jesuses that I have served and that have so deeply marked my life.

I'm at a fall camp with my church's youth group. I live for these moments, far from the family and the dark cloud that hangs over it. I'm amongst my tribe, with the pastor whom I admire. The framework is secure enough because of our shared faith, which makes proximity with girls possible. As close to paradise as I can imagine.

Every evening we get together to sing, watch a movie, play, hear a message. And after that, the pastor invites those who want to join him for a special moment of prayer to ask the Holy Spirit to come upon us. He calls it the upper room, referring to the place where the disciples of Jesus, after his resurrection, received the visitation of the Holy Spirit for the first time. I wouldn't miss it for the world.

Here we are, some of the most motivated, gathered around the pastor in a small dormitory. He explains to us what he calls "baptism in the Holy Spirit," a rite of passage typical of some evangelical churches. Those of us who ask for it will be filled with the presence of God and begin to speak in unknown and incomprehensible "tongues."

This will be the visible sign of this experience, and the entry into a new dimension of our Christian existence, filled with divine power and love in dimensions that ordinary Christians (those who were not "baptized in the Holy Spirit") cannot know.

It's an offer that cannot be refused! And I'm among the first to come forward to receive prayer. The pastor puts one hand on my head. The others, huddled around me, put their hands on my shoulders, on my back, on my neck. The pastor begins to pray, and he himself "speaks in tongues" while invoking the presence and action of Jesus within our small group. I feel so surrounded by this love. It merges with all this physical contact, this proximity, this warmth. There is something delightfully sensual and organic in this moment, and everything in me receives it. I try to open my mouth, but nothing comes. I try again, I pronounce a few syllables, hesitating, and finally the flow opens: I start to align sounds, unknown words, and I feel so good, most of all relieved... I've got it! This time God judged me worthy! Around me, tears and laughter. So close to each other, united by our shared emotion and by our bodies pressed against each other.

And the session continues until the end of the night: each in our turn, we receive this "baptism in the Holy Spirit." And the next day, the news spreads. Each evening, the ritual begins again, and others join us, then more people, until each person present at this camp, the cook included, has gone through this experience that we find so beautiful and so memorable.

Back home after the week away, a rumor spreads in the parish: the youth group had an experience of "spiritual awakening." The pastor takes the opportunity to consolidate his position and prestige among the council of elders who run the parish, and who don't all appreciate his theological orientations and plans for the church. As for me, I'm floating on a cloud. Finally, I have experienced something that reassures me not that God exists—that is a question that is not even allowed to be asked—but that I am one of the saved, the just, the elect.

Three decades later, I come across a childhood friend who was also at this camp, and whom I had lost sight of. We reflect on our memories and our journey as "unbelievers," we who have both turned our backs on this church, and I discover then how much some of the young people who attended this camp felt forced to participate in these moments, to the point of feigning the experience for fear of being excluded from the group and from its collective fervor.

I have long tried to protect this memory. It seemed so precious to me. I probably unconsciously wanted to preserve some kind of original purity. It was only when I spoke with this childhood friend that I realized fully the ambiguity of the experience during this camp. By putting this memory into words for this book, I see of course the adolescent aspiration towards an authentic spiritual experience. I also see the human warmth and sensuality of which I was so deprived. It could at least find a sort of outlet, in this proximity of mixed bodies and shared elation. But I also see the raw abuse, hidden behind the scenes, and the emerging fanaticism that would later take up so much space in my existence.

I am talking about abuse, and an abuse that was all the more effective since it was committed in all sincerity: the sincerity of this pastor, first, who offered us an experience in which he deeply believed. He did not realize that he was using us to confirm in his own eyes the religious system which also imprisoned him. I understood years later how it allowed him to distance his own emotional pain, including his repressed homosexuality. And then our group sincerity, so enthusiastic and proud to promote what we had experienced that it became impossible to evade it for anyone who wanted to rub shoulders with us. Anyone who wanted to continue to belong to our group had to live it, even if it meant pretending and reluctantly submitting to what had become the compulsory rite of passage.

This experience fed my nascent fanaticism: this "speaking in tongues" had become a foundation of my spirituality, so precious that nothing had the right to bring it into question. It validated the theology and the claims of this pastor who had thus claimed such authority over me. It thus made me immune to questioning and reinforced my need to convince others. I wanted them to enter into the belief system to which I fully subscribed, convinced that this was the best thing that could happen to them. It gave me an assurance that I had hitherto lacked, a kind of confirmation from the inside that I was indeed one of the elect and the "saved."

There is no sexual abuse in this memory, no apparent violence, no financial extortion. And yet all of the dynamics of abuse are present: there is the asymmetric relationship between an adult and adolescents, which allows the establishment of a relationship of power and domination. There are the pent-up needs and emotional failings of the victims, which create vulnerability and submission in the hope of gaining the attention and approval from the one who is seen as a benevolent parent figure. There are the hidden wounds and frailties of the perpetrator, which make him insensitive to the violence he exerts. Then there is the group, which reproduces the abuse suffered by imposing it on others. This is an example of spiritual abuse. It is subtler and less easy to recognize than other grosser abuses, but it is an abuse and toxic and harmful nonetheless.

The history of the Christian church is sadly littered with abuses of all kinds. This is not surprising, considering the dynamics of oppression and tyranny highlighted in the previous chapter. This is how **Jesus the enabler**, who covers up abuses, appears. Quite naturally, the toxic Jesus who oppresses men and women and empowers tyrants also provides cover for any kind of abuse perpetrated against those who endure his domination.

It's no wonder that so many sexual abuses have been

unveiled in the contemporary Church. The submission to tyranny of any kind leads to the understatement—and even dramatical concealment—of abuses. The victims of exposed abuse are unlikely to admit the gravity of what has been perpetrated against them, even more so the authorities to whom those crimes are occasionally reported.

In the name of Jesus, one person finds excuses for the perpetrator, another diminishes the gravity of the damage and negates the pain of the victim. Others shame and blame the victims for what they went through. Still others offer financial compensation on the condition that everything remains hidden, depriving victims of due justice for the sake of an institution's reputation. This whole context creates a climate where abuses are still likely to flourish and remain hidden for too long.

One other kind of abuse is spiritual abuse: when spiritual authority is used to establish one's power over another, be it to obtain money, prestige, obedience, or any kind of advantage. It may seem subtler, but in fact, it deeply harms those who suffer it, devastating many lives. This kind of abuse has been pervasive throughout all Church history and takes place in every Christian denomination.

Of course, the toxic Jesus also teaches us to ignore or minimize the abuses that we suffered in the intimacy of our education, life history and relationships.

People who are disempowered, ashamed of who they are physically, psychologically and spiritually, need to rely on strong external support: they need strong beliefs and absolute certitude. Anybody believing differently becomes a threat, any different worldview is unbearable.

This is called fanaticism, another face of the toxic Jesus: **Jesus the fanatic,** who supports extremism and violence. The fanatic sees a very clear line. On one side are the saved ones, the true believers, and on the other side are the lost, the nonbelievers and the wicked. In the best case, the nonbelievers must be convinced to come to the right side of the line and be saved, joining the flock of the righteous. In the worst case, they must be condemned, sometimes even slaughtered and sent to hell. In fact, this is what the fanatic Jesus plans to do at the end of times, or when he returns at any moment, according to various apocalyptic scenarios. Meanwhile, he encourages his followers to convert as many nonbelievers as they can.

The more or less intense presence of fanaticism at the root of their belief is one reason why many conservative Christian circles place such an importance on conversion. When even one person changes his or her belief or worldview and becomes part of the group, it's the subject of intense joy and relief for the whole group. The foundation of both the joy and the relief is not so much abstract love for this person who escaped perdition as it is the perceived strengthening of the group's own beliefs and certitude, the validation of their fanatical worldview.

I remember the moment I finally rebelled against the god of this Jesus, and I am grateful to the man I was at that time for his courage, because it was a decisive step in my long path towards greater freedom and integrity:

I am still a pastor, I still believe and feel part of the evangelical family, and yet I have reached a decisive stage. I have the feeling that my faith is becoming schizophrenic: on the one hand, I preach a god of love, who gives grace and who wants humans to be happy and free, and on the other hand, wherever I look, I see guilt, repression, and pain.

You must give the church "the tithe" or one-tenth of your revenue (at least!). One must be "sure of the will of God" before engaging in any project. Any personal decision risks being an expression of "the flesh" as the autonomous, and therefore necessarily sinful, will of the human. All joy and pride expose the sin of vanity. During the coun-selling sessions that are part of my pastor's work, I see the sexual misery, suffering, inhibitions, violence, and abuse that my parish-ioners suffer or perpetuate. They hide behind smiling faces and hands raised to the sky during Sunday praise.

Fear is everywhere. The society that surrounds us is nothing but a vast trap that tries to divert true Christians from the right path. They are children, so weak and so easily influenced. The church is the only refuge, and Christian rock bands, activities, and schools must be created so that young people do not turn away from it, fasci-nated by all that "the world" could offer them.

I have to recognize that it is the same in my own existence, marriage, and relationship with life and myself.

I'm starting to feel uneasy about letting my children go to "Sunday School" since my six-year-old son came home crying. The instructor (a brave woman who couldn't be more kind and lovely to children) told him that characters from Pokemon, a game he loves, are demons in disguise and that this game should be absolutely banned.

It takes grace, in fact, to absorb so much guilt, so much fear. It takes nothing less than the blood and suffering of the cross to allow this terrorized people to live as best as they can under the gaze of such a stern god.

This is, I think, the first time I have dared to make a free choice based on what my heart said to me. I can no longer ignore everything I see around me. I carry within me the tenuous, but very present, intu-ition of a divine who welcomes me as I am and invites me to life and free-dom. I no longer want to try to reconcile all this crap with this intuition.

I remember very well the moment when I made this choice between the severe god and the divine of my intuition. It was during a time of personal devotion, a compulsory practice for Evangelicals. I remember the mixture of audacity and terror that inhabited me when I said, in a sort of prayer: "This God I don't want, and if I'm wrong and he sends me to hell, I would rather go than submit to him."

I never suspected when I said these words that they were going to lead me so far and open a path for me to get out of the personal hell in which I indeed was.

Unfortunately, fanatical thinking and behavior is not the exception throughout Church history, nor even in current Christianity. Every period of Christian history is crisscrossed by violence, be it against people of other beliefs or among Christian groups believing differently. Even today in Russia, we witness a massive revival of the Orthodox religion, together with nationalism and integrism. It is encouraged by political authorities, who view it as a kind of a cement for a renewed Russian society, proud of their Christian history. This trend fosters violent action against homosexuals, feminists, and people who practice other religions.

In several parts of the world, among them the USA and Brazil, "born again" Christians constitute a political force able to influence the results of major elections. Unfortunately, most of the time their votes are captured by politicians promoting different kinds of intolerance and repression.

These days, Catholicism seems to be less prone to fanatical violence or radical politics; perhaps it is too busy with sexual abuse scandals. But not so long ago some conservative parts of the Catholic Church were supporting some of the bloodiest and most repressive dictators in the world.

All in the name of Jesus, of course.

Arriving at the end of this chapter, most of what I feel is heaviness and sadness.

What a mess!

How is it possible that so much toxicity has been created in the name of a sincere and loving man, who many believe was an enlightened master or even the son of God, whose dedicated followers tried their best to understand his deep spiritual teaching and to live and continue his message?

Here is the last toxic Jesus who appears through my memories: **Jesus Frankenstein.** He truly gave birth to monsters!

Let me be very clear that I'm not attacking Christianity in particular. For some readers, your toxic Jesuses may well be toxic Buddhas, Krishnas, gurus, Allahs or Jehovahs, even toxic Gaias or other goddesses. Nor am I attacking religion or spirituality in general. What needs to be emphasized most strongly is our vulnerability to their deceptive faces, caused by the very human tendency, common to all of us, to bypass and repress our deepest wounds and fears.

And of course, the more we are wounded, the more we need care, respect and love to face and integrate past traumas, neglect, or harmful education. In searching for some caring or answers, we may be particularly subject to toxic beliefs, hoping to find relief in them, but in the end only bypassing what needs to be faced directly, possibly with the help of a good therapist.

This repression doesn't happen because we are flawed or lazy, but because the traumas that caused the wounds happened to us at times in our development when we were not at all able to cope with them. Neither were our parents or the adults in charge able to reassure and help us.

This caused something to become frozen in us, creating numbness and dark shadows where toxicity and insanity can easily grow, far away from our awareness. Religion and spirituality too often become excellent hideouts where we can disguise, bypass, or avoid facing what is hidden and growing in those dark places.

I'm deeply convinced of the value of true spirituality as a necessary part of a full human experience. I'm also convinced that nobody comes to spirituality without carrying in one way or another some toxic beliefs, living in shadows that need enlightenment in order to find the freedom and space to grow and heal.

That's the essential condition necessary to live a spiritual journey that gives all the fruits that we can expect from it—fruits of maturity, freedom, compassion, integration, and hopefully an authentic connection with the Great Mystery. And that's the subject of the next part of this book.

PART II

AND GRACE...FINALLY!

7

DISCOVERING MY OWN PERSONAL JESUS

I 'm 54 years old. I'm waiting with my wife for what should be a routine appointment with my doctor. My leg had sponta-neously broken again, revealing the illusion of my "healing" some forty years ago. Six weeks ago the doctor had repaired it with some titanium pieces, and now I'm recovering quite well. We enter the doctor's office, and I begin to feel a lump in my throat as I see his solemn expression.

"It's totally unexpected," he says. "It almost never happens." The routine bone analysis after my surgery has revealed a rare cancer. He needs to do further examinations to decide exactly what to do. But in any case the situation will require surgery and possibly amputation.

We return home, my wife and I, in a state of shock. She tells me about an intuition she has that we need to rely on Christ's energy to receive help and protection in this impossible situation. Strangely, this revelation meets my own inner feeling: the week before, at a Yoga training we both attended, I had been moved to tears talking with a scholar in Tantric Hinduism and discovering many common points between what he was describing about the relationship between Shiva and Shakti, at the origin of everything, and some of what I *knew about Jesus and his Father from my Christian background. It had awakened in me the desire to reconnect with this Jesus to whom I had been so dedicated, but in a new and freer way.*

The night comes. Impossible to sleep, of course. Terror prowls around the fringe of my consciousness. What is going to happen? How am I going to cope with it? And Evelise? The tension is unbearable. So I do what I learned and practiced for many years in meditation: I let it all be here, not trying to repress anything or change what I'm feeling and thinking, and I begin to anchor my attention on my breathing and watch the turmoil inside me. And very spontaneously I do something I had never done before: I concentrate on the word "Jesus" and use it as a mantra. Jesus inhale, Jesus exhale. To my great surprise, I feel overwhelmed by peace and by a deep trust that I'm not alone and will be able to face this situation. I sleep quietly for the rest of the night.

This mantra stays with me in the weeks to come, and every time I use it (which has been very often) the peace comes back—when I'm interacting with the doctors, when I'm faced with difficult decisions, before my amputation, during the recovery process.

Under urgent doctor's orders the following day: scanner, MRI, analysis of the results.

And good and bad news. The good: no metastasis in the rest of my body, which gives me a chance to be cured and live further. The bad: the cancer has spread from my bone, growing in a soft-tissue sarcoma that is progressively invading my thigh. The treatment that gives me the best chances of long-term survival, but still with no guarantee, is the amputation of my whole leg up to the hip.

I listen to the doctors discussing my case and their different options. Part of me is breathing, repeating my new mantra. Their faces express some surprise when I immediately declare, "Let's do this amputation without delay. I want to live!"

The surgery happens some days later, on May 31st. Right before I receive the anesthesia, I commit my life to Jesus, with the deep feeling that I'm going to the underworld, and that He has been there before me and goes with me on this journey. I wake up without my leg, but still with that peace, which never leaves me in the coming days.

One point I need to make: that peace hasn't meant there wasn't sadness, grief, fear, anger, anxiety. All those feelings have been present, sometimes invasive, sometimes threatening. But in a mysterious way, that peace was present with me in the foreground, providing a kind of rest and refuge in the midst of the turmoil, a safe place where I knew I could come back every time I needed it.

To my own astonishment and that of the medical team, one day after the amputation I'm out of intensive care, and one week later I've recovered enough to go back home. Four weeks later I'll be on a plane to Oregon to participate in the therapy group described earlier. We had planned the trip months ahead, but I thought it would be impossible due to the circumstances. Fortunately, it wasn't, since the trip turned out to be so important in helping me process all of these events and go through this dramatic phase of my life.

This mystical or spiritual experience—I don't know what to name it—has been a pivotal point in my life journey. First it gave me the help I needed to face and go through what was happening to me. It still does. But its effects went way beyond that.

I had never experienced a sense of such a helping and loving presence, coming to my rescue in that tragic moment, and that presence clearly had the identity of Jesus. I had spent my childhood, teenage and many years of my adult life praying to him, reading about him, preaching about him, longing for him, trying my best to believe in him and to be his true disciple, but in all that time I had never had even a glimpse of what was happening to me now. Yes, I had sometimes felt moments of love and peace, and I had been moved and uplifted by what I knew about him. But this feeling was beyond what I ever felt. Now he *was here* totally unexpectedly. It was not a question of effort or belief. He was simply here and his felt presence was helping me in a way that I couldn't have even hoped or imagined. Whenever I thought of it I could only cry and revel in this peace and this love I was feeling deep inside, and be grateful.

But what was this experience? Was it a kind of enlightenment, or was it a relapse to my evangelical upbringing, a regression to a childish way of relating to reality under the pressure of these terrible circumstances? Looking back, I can paradoxically say it was both. It was an authentic spiritual experience, coming from the most luminous place to help me in my desperate need. And it was coming in a form that would bring me face to face with the spiritual toxicity that was remaining hidden in the depth of my psyche.

I used the phrase "pivotal point" because this experience produced more than the support I needed to face the terrifying situation I was in. It produced a shift in my consciousness, a kind of waking up. I began to consider my whole inner world in a new perspective, in a slow and progressive inner process that is still unfolding as I write these lines.

At first I noticed that a strong desire to live was arising in me, due in part to my debilitated, life-threatening situation. But it was also very clear that this presence was sustaining and encouraging that desire to live, and more precisely, focusing it or part of it.

Then this new light shining into my life had a strange and paradoxical effect: a bit like when you move a stone and you can see the insects and worms who were hiding under it begin to panic and crawl in all directions under the disturbing light. The creatures were of course all the toxic Jesuses I have described.

The first person who was able to see them clearly was my dear Evelise: she began to address some of my behaviors and brought them up during that therapy week. And very soon it was as if the pieces of the puzzle I had tried to assemble during many years were coming together much quicker than before. I could begin to see more and more clearly the big picture: the toxic Jesuses and their demands and influence in my life; the sweet Jesus who was meeting me in such a tender way, and his discrete presence all along my history. I began to see the difference between them: the ugliness and arrogance of the toxic Jesuses; the humility and simplicity of the luminous presence.

I need to say more about the process that led me to open my eyes finally to these evil creatures. Indeed, they had so deeply conditioned my relationship with life that I almost gave in to their poisonous seduction, even as I was beginning to untie the threads of toxic spirituality gripping me.

Let me tell you how I woke up in extremis, thanks to the help of my wife, even when this death song was about to hypnotize me again:

We are on the eve of our departure for the therapy group in Oregon. The future looks so uncertain, the present so threatening. And yet, I feel like I am on a cloud. I feel uplifted by my spiritual experience, which greatly supported me to face the appalling difficulties of the preceding weeks, which I will speak about in more detail in another chapter. Every time I think about it, I feel this peace and the presence of my friend Jesus, and tears come to my eyes.

But the pain is there: the daily frustration of waking up each day with only one leg, the injections of anticoagulant each evening, the phantom pains and those following the surgery that wake me up at night and torment me during the day, and the powerful painkillers to avoid a vicious circle of chronic pain. Of course, the significant risk of the cancer reoccurring bothers me and my wife as well as the prospect of checks that will have to be carried out every three months. My spiritual experience took me by surprise and came to support my life energy and courage. It gave me the strength to face the situation. But beside it, another more insidious voice tries to creep in.

In the evening, with a certain pride in being in such a state of

*serenity and spiritual elevation, I say to Evelise: "You know, with this
presence of Jesus at my side, I now feel ready to face everything
peacefully, even if I were to die, even if the cancer came back." To my
surprise, she looks troubled. We talk about it the next day, and she
tells me about her anger and her concern. She hates this resignation.
She understands if I am tired of living with everything I endure, but
for her part, she is not tired of my presence at her side and if it
happened that cancer comes back, she would prefer to see me rebel-
lious, furious, harassing doctors to find the best treatment, and stir-
ring up and down to try to counter the threat. I am very touched by
these words. They instill in me a saving discomfort.*

*I return to Evelise's reaction in my head. What should I think of
my experience? Deep down, I feel the urge to live, the rage even, but I
cannot deny that this prospect of an unshakable and heroic serenity,
even in suffering and in death, awakens in me a strong echo, even
seduces me somehow. What to do with all this?*

*The time to leave for Oregon arrives, and we go to the airport: the
big one-legged man with crutches, barely recovered from his amputation, pockets full of painkillers, to try to make the 12 hour flight bear-
able, and the little Brazilian girl, 1m58, on the verge of tears, with the
burden of two large suitcases and her disabled husband.*

*The trip is going better than we had expected. I manage to steal a
few moments of respite for my scar by lying on the floor on a blanket
between the two hostesses' passages, and I finally suffer only a little.
We arrive in Oregon and start the therapy group. I talk about the
religious environment in which I grew up, the so-called miraculous
healing of my leg, my years of pastoral commitment, my revolts and
my questioning, and then the illness that affects me and the spiritual
experience that accompanied it. I feel the group is very impressed, of
course, and the therapist is a little taken aback. With his help, I listen
to my emotions, my physical feelings, my anger, and my pain. In the
evening, in the hotel's happily deserted swimming pool, Evelise and I
find ourselves in hot water and suddenly a dyke breaks in me. I start
to sob in her arms. I give free rein to my pain and anger.*

The next day in the group, it is again the anger that rises in me. As the day progresses, it turns into rage, vital energy, and revolt. Little by little, the pieces of the puzzle are put in place with relentless clarity until a window suddenly opens during a moment of inner exploration under the guidance of the therapist.

I hear like never before the part of me that harasses me, accusing me and locking me up. This inner persecutor repeats over and over in the back of my mind: "You should be strong; you should do more; you should have more faith; you should be more spiritual. You're a failure; you're not doing enough; you're unable. You should be heroic. You'll never be enough. You deserve shaming. You should disappear; you should take less space; you should sacrifice yourself; you should be more like Jesus; you should be submissive. You are little; you are insignificant." With these voices, the light shines on the toxic Jesuses. I see them all clearly, in a kind of upside down epiphany.

And I hear another voice full of rage crying in me:"I DON'T WANT TO BE LIKE JESUS, I WANT TO BE ME. I DON'T WANT TO SACRIFICE. I WANT TO LIVE. I WANT TO HEAL. I DON'T WANT TO DIE. I REFUSE TO ACCEPT AND RESIGN TO WHAT HAPPENS TO ME. I WANT TO TAKE CARE OF MYSELF. I DON'T NEED JESUS. I NEED ME." I know it's my most authentic voice, and I feel deep inside that that voice resonates in harmony with the spiritual experience that carried me through the ordeal.

I see and feel what is deeply healthy about its experience. I see how it has carried me through the drama of the past few weeks, how it has sustained my vital energy and given me the courage, anger, and clarity that I needed to face it. At the same time, I feel how different the prospect of a fool proof serenity is that I had shared with Evelise. I see how it feeds on my unhealthy inner speech and expresses the toxic forces that have been at work in my education and life. I see how these forces tried to piggyback on the experience that helped me, to place themselves under their patronage and subvert, parasitize, and vampirize it. I discover the toxic Jesuses who want death, resignation, passivity, and suffering and with them, the procession of all the others, born of buried wounds and denied suffering.

This is where this book was born. All of its content are just the unfolding of what happened in this intense moment of awareness.

Here it's important to re-emphasize the importance of my relationship with my soul-partner. I'll never be grateful enough for this relationship, in which we are able to encourage each other, to share love, security and care, while at the same time offering each other confronting views and challenging observations in a safe place. All of this created opportunities for growing and maturing.

I must also reiterate her intuition in relating to Christ consciousness and returning to our Christian roots, which met my own intuition and strengthened it so much. In addition, she possessed the perspicacity to notice, and the courage to express, her uneasiness with some manifestations of the toxic Jesuses that she could see showing up in me, trying to take advantage of my spiritual experience and subvert it. In our group therapy this perception was elaborated and processed with the contribution of the participants and the insights of the therapist. It all gave me the impetus to enter into the process of clearing and revisiting my history in a new light, which unfolded in the weeks and months that followed and resulted in the whole spectrum of clarity and consciousness that I recount in this book.

Jesus my Guruji

After having left my former job as a pastor, I entered resolutely into a part of my life where I enjoyed my new freedom of doubting, of asking questions, of reconsidering every belief I had. First I left any form of spirituality. But soon I had to acknowledge that I couldn't help being strongly interested in that subject, and I began to discover new ways to explore it.

First I learned to meditate in a very secular tradition: the mindfulness protocol developed by Jon Kabat-Zinn. I did a ten-week program, then built a personal practice, then jumped at the chance of completing a one-year training program in that discipline for a Certificate of Advanced Studies created by the University of Geneva and the State Hospital. At the same time, I was discovering Yoga, thanks to Evelise, and the importance of the body in any spiritual practice. I became Catholic like her, in order to keep a bond with Christianity, where my roots are, but in a tradition where the importance of the ritual and the place left to silence was allowing me to participate in a way that wasn't possible any more for me in Evangelical or Protestant churches. I explored Hinduism, yogic meditation, mantras and mudras, and the powerful mythology behind each. I was struck by the way the different gods and goddesses are expressions of the divine energies of the universe, and how all those energies are present and active inside every one of us. I practiced Bon Buddhist meditation and could touch the silence and clear light that reside at the core of reality.

Through all these explorations, time after time, I was impressed by that strong feeling that all of these different practices and religions, though contradictory and different as they appear, were just imperfect ways for human beings to account for their experience of reality and of the divine, the great mystery, whatever you want to name it. Each deserved to be listened to and respected, in the same way that they all needed to be questioned, since they had the potential to become toxic and repressive.

When I experienced the presence of Jesus in my deepest need, it gave me the impulse and the light I needed to come back to my Christian roots and to reconsider that heritage that was so much a part of me. I needed to clean up the mess left by the dark part of that heritage, while reconnecting with the part that had been life-sustaining and healthy. In doing that, I realized how much help I could receive from my new and wider perspective and all the treasures I had discovered through those other traditions and practices.

There is a notion in Hinduism that struck me as very accurately describing this new relationship between me and Jesus: the notion of the Guru.

The Guru is a twofold reality. First there is the inner Guru: the part of me that is very clear, in contact with my inner light, and free from all restriction, illusion and coercion. My better self, unfortunately, is rarely able to manifest without interference and coverup. Meditation and spiritual practice are about discovering that inner Guru and tuning into him more and more, becoming who we really were from the beginning.

Second are the outer Gurus, the people who can become for us the masters, able to lead us on that path of connecting with and following our inner Guru. Of course, the outer Guru can generate many abuses. We all know many examples.

But in my situation, I realized quite spontaneously that through this new encounter with Jesus, I had found my Guru, or my Guruji—"ji" is a Sanskrit suffix expressing tender love and gratefulness, so, "my sweet beloved master." This is how Mary Magdalene greeted Jesus when she faced Him alive again: "Rabbouni!" she exclaimed, which translates from the Aramaic exactly the same.

Jesus as my Guruji is the one who leads me on the path of discovering and connecting with that part of me that is enlightened, connected with the divine, or to put it in Jesus's own words, with the kingdom of God that resides within us.

My Guruji is here to help me to become more who I really am, free from the tyranny, the illusion, the fears that constitute the different layers of my false egos, that alienate me from my innermost self. I can really trace that grace through my whole life. It has given me a solid perspective so that I can distinguish between the toxic parts of my religious heritage—all the toxic Jesuses—and the light helping me to find my way through life's difficulties.

What I Can Say about Jesus

My Jesus is a master of wisdom at the highest level. He values my experience, my feelings and my intelligence, and wants me to make good use of them and develop them. He encourages me to grow to full sensitivity and consciousness, to be more finely tuned into my inner world of emotions, impulses, body sensations and intuition. He teaches me to know myself and to use my intelligence, together with that inner knowing, to perceive and deal with reality more accurately. He wants me to ask questions, raise doubts, welcome and listen to disturbing facts.

He firmly insists that I don't submit passively to life's obstacles and that I don't choose the "easy way" of fatalism and resignation. He enjoys seeing me grow and mature, more able to face with dignity and relevance the different challenges of life. He is himself a master of the fine art of navigation in the sea of reality, and makes me his proud apprentice in the same art, planting in my deepest being the resolve to make the best of my life.

As I write these lines, all kinds of memories come back to me that remind me that this Jesus has long been present by my side, inviting me to come out of the drowsiness and hardening caused by my toxic environment:

I have been a pastor for almost fifteen years. I have been going from questioning to questioning for several years, without having rejected either my evangelical faith or my vocation. I still have the impression that I can invite my brothers and sisters to live their faith in a freer and healthier way.

My preaching opens more and more space for questions. I'm publishing an article for the church newspaper called "Do we really have to be fundamentalists?" I dare to write that the Holy Spirit acts far beyond the borders of the church and even influences the "non-Christians" who love the truth. I even invite my parishioners to let themselves be enriched by their contribution and to listen to the voice of the Spirit in what we call "the world," that is to say everything that is not the evangelical church.

I remember long discussions with Alain, who I met following an evangelizing action that I organized in the streets of the city. He had been drawn to the prospect of discussing the Bible, a book he was curious about despite his professed atheism. He had founded a meeting of Alcoholics Anonymous in Geneva, having himself overcome morbid alcoholism. I am struck by the story of his life change: I find in it all the traditional elements of an evangelical "conversion," but without Jesus, the Bible, or the church. What to do with it?

I'm starting therapy. I take liberties. I join a boxing and full contact club.

I dare to take up questions shyly that I had stifled during my theological studies. I am increasingly struck by the different visions of god and faith that I find in the stories of the Bible that I continue to read daily. Instead of trying daring pirouettes to reconcile them, I come to realize that I have to choose: who is the god I want? The Jesus I choose? How to live the faith? It is only from this choice, and therefore from this freedom, that I can interpret these texts.

Until the day when, during a session, I announce to my therapist that I have decided to give my leave. I realize that my function as pastor does not give me the freedom I need to fully explore the questions that have opened up in me. I'm going to take the plunge, announce to my parish council that I'm resigning, and start looking for work for the first time in my life.

I'm a little annoyed by her reaction: "Finally! It's not too soon!"

When I get home, I feel dizzy. What is in store for me? Am I going too far? And yet, I feel deep inside me a little voice, that of Jesus it seems to me, that whispers to me: "Go ahead. I'm with you. It's time for you to grow up and let go of my hand, to dare to walk alone!"

My Guruji is a powerful healer, a fountain of life energy, resolutely dedicated to life and always prone to sustain it, and to give me comfort, or relieve my pain and suffering. He doesn't ignore pain or death, in fact he faced them both and passed through them in a way that most humans won't have to experience. He knows them from the inside out and takes them very seriously, but is not fascinated by them. It's for love that he faced sacrifice and suffering, in order to remain faithful to his calling and his innermost being, but he doesn't value them for their own sake.

When I was confronting my darkest hours, having to face illness, death and amputation, he was there, very close to me. He sustained my life energy, comforting me and giving me peace and courage to face my journey through the underworld. I knew that he wouldn't leave me on this path. Now he inspires in me a deep love for life and a desire for living, coming from the depth of my being, even stronger now that I know better that death and pain may be part of life at any moment. When I look with him at the world and at my existence, he strengthens my innate joy, curiosity, awe and compassion.

My Master is a great enlightened being. He dared to claim his own divinity and total unity with God, shocking and angering dedicated and religious people of his time so much that they wanted to kill him. He revealed to his disciples, and still does, their own divinity, and showed them how to access the kingdom of God by emptying themselves of their pretensions and pride, and seeking silence and solitude. In that place of silence comes learning: to discover God, the Great Mystery and the kingdom of God; to open up to others; to see the simplicity and beauty of the present moment; to sense the Immediate Presence dwelling within all reality. For me, meditating in his presence is eye-opening and thought-clarifying. Simply breathing while repeating his name is a practice that helps me dissipate the veil of worry and the repetitive-thinking mind, focus on what really matters, and align my life to it. And I keep on learning.

In that process my Jesus encourages me to value, enjoy, and cherish my freedom and to get rid of every tyranny, thus sharing with me his own freedom. He gives me a beautiful example of masculinity, fully integrating his feminine side, loving, respecting and empowering women and men as well. He constantly encourages me to cherish simple life pleasures, relationships and love.

He is open-minded and shows the deepest respect for practitioners of every religion, and for the nonreligious as well. He shares with them the same humanity. He was and is always ready to engage in deep conversation with any sincere seeker. He gives me full clearance to do the same and to let me be informed and enriched in this exercise, free to learn from others, as well as to share my own experience and perspective.

What I Mean by "My Own Personal Jesus"

When I use the words "my own personal Jesus," I don't mean in any way that Jesus is like my property or my servant or any such thing. I also don't mean a kind of little Jesus of my creation whom I can use or shape as I wish, or who can be the projection of my needs, desires and good "spiritual" ideas.

Jesus is who he is. He is a historical person whose existence, teaching and death have been objectively attested, and he is now part of another realm of existence since his death and what his disciples witnessed as his resurrection. From this realm he lives and acts in completely different ways than living human beings. He exists over and beyond objectivity and is supremely free. He is no person's, religion's or movement's property or subject. He is over and beyond what anybody can imagine, believe or conceive, as much as he is over and beyond any belief, dogma, creed or speculation.

But when he connects with me, when he enters into a relationship and even a friendship with me, the result is unique: "my own personal" relationship with him. Bringing his respect, love and compassion, he meets me in the places of my deepest needs. Thus my relationship with him takes on a special quality, a specific color. I'm especially sensitive to particular aspects of his person, some parts of his teaching, that dovetail with my own history, my deepest wounds and unique sensibility. This all shapes a very intimate relationship, always evolving and refining itself.

It doesn't mean that Jesus will be another Jesus for another person, but this other person will have a different relationship with him and perceive and value different aspects of him. In fact there is so much richness in Jesus's personality that there will also be an immense variety of relationships with him inside and outside Christianity, sometimes with large differences among them, depending on specific life histories and belief systems.

From this perspective, the community that gathers around Jesus through time and space provides an opportunity to discover what others perceive about Him and what kind of relationship they have with Him. If embraced openly, the sharing of divergent perspectives and experiences by sincere spiritual seekers promotes growth and evolution and eventually the discernment needed to purge projections and expectations that so often give birth to the toxic Jesuses and other toxic expressions of spirituality.

I experienced this community in the most unexpected, paradoxical, and, as it seems, the least "Christian" environment that can be imagined while I was on a strange pilgrimage that led me to the mists of Avalon:

We are a little over a year before the health problems that led to my amputation and all the changes and discoveries that I relate in this book.

For more than a year, Evelise has participated in an online training course called "urban priestess." I regularly see her perform strange rituals by turning to the four cardinal points, interacting online with "sisters" around the world, and reconciling with the cycles of nature and those of her female body. I also see her flourish, develop her intuition in an amazing way, overcome fears that were making her life difficult, gain confidence like never before, and develop her spirituality with a depth and freedom that I find beautiful and utterly inspiring.

Therefore, I do not hesitate very long when she invites me to participate with her in a kind of initiatory journey that is part of this training. So here we are on our way to Glastonbury, England, a small town that attracts like a magnet a motley gathering of hippies and mystics of all kinds. Here, the legends of King Arthur and the fairy Morgana still live in the land of the mythical mists of Avalon.

We arrive where the retreat will take place. It is a complex of medieval houses away from the city, a vast area of organic vegetable and medicinal plants gardens, sacred groves, even a circle of magic trees. There is an atmosphere of mystery. The place is restored and animated by a strange character: a mixture of entrepreneur, hermit, and eccentric scientist and a great lover of myths, legends, and esotericism.

I find myself in the midst of a group of around 30 witches, priestesses, and magicians from all over the world, including my wife, as well as a few men. I will spend a week with them listening to myths, participating in rituals, and visiting sacred places. If I had a premonitory vision 10 years ago of the places my decisions would take me, I probably would have believed myself to be hallucinating.

Yet, I lived moments that helped me to reconnect resolutely with spirituality and started on me a process of reconciliation with my history. This was also a process of liberation. I see it clearly today as an important step towards the healing and integration journey that I went through a few months later, which are the subject of this book, and towards the awareness that allowed me to confront what was toxic in my relationship with life and spirituality.

But let's go back to the mists of Avalon. My first movement is of slight distrust. Since I left the evangelical church, I don't feel comfortable in groups, whatever they are. I am too afraid to find the dynamics that I have left, like gregarious submission to a common way of thinking, conformism, and the repression of doubt and intelligence in favour of belief.

I am also wary of spirituality, even though it continues to attract me. Of course, I practice mindfulness meditation and yoga. I sit from time to time alone in a church, burning a candle in front of a statue of the Virgin or Christ and meditating in silence. Yet, I remain ambivalent and hurt. It is difficult for me to speak without irony or bitterness about my past as an evangelical pastor and Christian or even about my interest in spirituality. I feel that I should not throw away everything, but I don't know what to do with this part of my life.

I gradually let myself be tamed by the free and warm climate that reigns in this colorful band, and I meet beautiful people there.

There is Ian, traumatized and outraged by the racism and violence he experienced in South Africa, where he grew up, and by the way the church vouched for the abominations he witnessed. In paganism, he found a space for freedom that allowed him to overcome these painful experiences and live a spirituality that carries him, especially when mourning his wife died the year before. It is in memory of her that he made this trip.

There is Kristen, priestess, magician, and astrologer. During a shared meal, I discover how her life course is the opposite of mine, and I feel much respect for the wisdom and maturity she accumulated and for the constancy and freedom with which she explored the paths of spirituality.

There is Alexandra, blonde and diaphanous, who is only missing *wings or we would take her for a fairy (by the way, fairies are considered very seriously in this circle). The day before my amputation, she will send me an image of Jesus walking on water in the middle of the storm, making me sure of her prayers.*

There is Nancy, a wise woman, who will reveal a year later consistency and generosity that still move me today. Throughout the duration of my hospitalization and my recovery, she writes every day with little messages of encouragement, sweet and sensitive. She prays and does rituals for my healing and for Evelise. She is part of a supportive circle that has grown around us from all over the world. This encourages me and Evelise enormously. I am convinced that this contributed concretely to my recovery.

I also discover that behind rituals, stories, and what look to me like exotic beliefs, there is intelligence, freedom, poetry, and a way of using myth and magic to open up to dimensions of reality and of one's own humanity which outgrow pure rationality.

Here I am walking barefoot on the land of legends, meditating among the sacred trees. I am listening to what an apple tree in the circle of sacred trees might have to say to me, chanting mantras while turning towards the four cardinal points, and crying all the tears of my body while hearing a flamboyant old hippie witch playing a drum and leading us in a shamanic experience. I feel like a fish in water. I feel change occurring inside of me. I cannot define it, but I open up, relax, have fun, and take advantage of this environment and freedom.

I remember my teenage love for fantasy and science fiction: The Lord of the Rings that I read and reread and that was so dear to my heart, The Nine Princes in Amber and their psychedelic tarot deck, and the poster of Roger Dean with a six-armed mage meditating in front of a mysterious city. I had pinned the poster up in my room despite its obvious contradictions to the evangelical shackles which enclosed me. I find the Marc-Henri of that time who was trying to use the imaginary to create space. He feels good here. After having *suffocated for decades, he breathes air, giving him strength and pleasure.*

One day, we visit the white source, the source of the sacred masculine. This is a high place in these magic lands. The warden opens the door to a dark cave, in which several pools collect the icy water from the spring. All around are various erected altars, sacred images honoring the Stag God, and ritual objects made of branches, glassware, ribbons, and candles. I feel like I'm in a hippie museum, a punk cathedral, a delirium of raw art, a space between this world and another.

The day before, Sianna, who leads this retreat and signs the preface to this book, spoke brilliantly about the traditions of the sacred masculine and feminine. These two dimensions of all being are symbolized by the two sources that flow in this land of Avalon, the red and the white. She evoked the myths of various traditions and notably summoned the figures of Christ and Mary Magdalene as great archetypes of the masculine and feminine. She invited us to seize these myths and let them speak to our depths, to reconnect with all of the dimensions of our being, including those that still remain hidden in the shadows out of shame or out of fear.

When the time comes, I strip naked in the dark without hesitation and enter black, icy waters. I meditate there for a moment with the other men in our group, then I immerse myself with them three times. I am intimately aware that I am self administering a new baptism. A baptism in my own humanity. A baptism in all parts of me that I have rejected and tried to deny. A baptism of openness to any experience that can make me grow and mature, to any tradition that brings light and truth, to all sincere human beings. A baptismal antidote to bigotry and fanaticism that have characterized so many years of my life. A baptism of reconciliation with myself, with my past. A baptism of integration and healing. A baptism in the Great Mystery of existence.

I come out of it freezing.

I also come out with something that will carry me beyond what I imagined: a viaticum, which will manifest itself in the form of aid received in my darkest moments and which will allow me to pass through the ordeal that awaits me. The viaticum is a portal to a more mature life and spirituality, richer, more integrated, and purged of its toxicity.

8

GRACE INDEED—BUT WHAT A FIERCE GRACE!

I say unto you:
one must still have chaos in oneself
to give birth to a dancing star.
—*Nietzsche, from "Thus spoke Zarathustra"*

A s I mentioned earlier, looking back on my journey I can identify a thread of grace running throughout every moment of my personal history despite all the toxicity I have described. It has been the lever, the ferment of the possibility for transformation that I have experienced in different periods of my development.

In retrospect I have found several stages to help highlight the nature and power of this grace.

1. The Stage of Unconsciousness

And not a happy-go-lucky unconsciousness! This is the unconsciousness of a child growing up in a difficult environment, having to cope with so many traps, hidden messages, threats and trauma that I had to numb, blind and harden myself. At this stage I was trying to adhere absolutely to my parents' beliefs and worldview, trying to please them as much as possible, misusing my intuition to guess their hidden needs and wounds and try my best to make them feel good. Mission impossible, of course, but a mission nonetheless, and one demanding the complete repression of my own needs.

This stage was about building the foundation of submission to tyranny and all the internal systems of self-denial that serve it. In my therapeutic work I would later give them names, like the inner critic and the inner saboteur, and learn to overcome their oppression. At the same time I would meet and comfort the terrified and oppressed child I was but could find only in some hidden place deep inside.

But this stage was also about grace working undercover, fighting a secret guerrilla war against the tyranny by planting seeds—of the desire for freedom, growth and autonomy—everywhere it could hide them. Grace protected those seeds as much as possible from extermination, in the expectation that some might flourish in the future and break the concrete barriers built year after year and trauma after trauma, hopefully preparing the moments of breakthrough, liberation and healing.

Let me be clear on this point: I don't know for sure where that grace comes from. Some will want to believe it comes from above, being a kind of supernatural expression of divine love. Some will prefer to consider it built into human nature, perhaps a reflexive survival instinct that can never completely renounce growth and healing and will not give in to alienation and asphyxia.

For me this question is not really relevant, and the answer could well be both, the inborn force being in my opinion one of the many expressions of the divine. Anyway, grace is and will always remain beyond any definition or explanation, free as it is in its very nature. What seems to me much more important is that I had to learn over time to welcome this grace, to work with it instead of resisting it and trying to repress it—to the point where I could finally dare to be myself, and become, for my own benefit, the carrier of this grace.

So, looking back, I discovered grace as this impulse in me that wants life and growth at any price:

- Grace as a subversive force, able to hide and disguise itself, working in the margins, working undercover.
- Grace as the seeds of discomfort, dissatisfaction and imbalance.
- Grace as the grains of sand that in the long run will sabotage the strong machinery of repression and persistent submission to tyranny.

2. The Stage of Necessary Decisions and their Consequences

There may come a moment when the seeds of grace begin to come to fruition. That moment for me was not easy or comfortable or peaceful.

In this stage grace manifested for me first as conflicts and dissatisfaction. Or, as I see it now, grace uncovered in me the ability, really the necessity, to face the increasingly unbearable presence of chronic suffering.

Grace first revealed and even created chaos and conflict while I was wearing the mask of perfection, order and harmony. I was trying hard to build an identity and a life project that would ease the inner conflicts born in my early life. I was working hard to find a kind of balance by being the perfect, submissive, smiling Christian, marrying the right girl, embracing the career of the good pastor. But grace was always there like the little stone in the shoe. You can try to ignore it for a while, you can pretend it doesn't hurt or it's not important, but the more you walk, the more you know that's not true.

So began a process of facing where I was uncomfortable and where I was repressing myself. This happened in a kind of spiraling way: beginning in the periphery, then going further and further towards the center.

The stone in the shoe at that time was my intimate relationship with my ex-wife, where it appeared more and more clearly that my numbness and difficulty to feel and act according to what was happening inside of me was problematic, and that my inner problems were making me insensitive, inadequate, and self-sabotaging. Add to this the normal challenges of family life and the deep emotional wounds of my ex-wife, and soon our shared sufferings and violent conflicts were becoming unbearable, driving both of us—first her, then me—to seek professional help.

In daring to face the realization that my life was at a dead end, the first point of focus was my religious belief system and my pastoral vocation. I acknowledged my integrism and tendency to fanaticism, and how they were fundamental tenets of the church I pastored. I became aware of the abuses I had been subjected to as a child, among them the "healing" I recounted earlier. I began to see the deep well of anxieties and wounds in my family and how my parents had used religion to protect themselves from them. And I realized that I was reproducing it in my own way, becoming the sustainer of a system that I was at the same time a victim of.

Then grace provided me with the courage to make difficult and necessary decisions and face the consequences: I resigned from my pastoral function and began to look for a secular job. This decision was the first in a process of liberation that happened during the coming years and still goes on.

It then took me almost ten years to face the fact that our

relationship couldn't be saved, for it was built too deeply on foundations of self-repression, self-destruction, and mutual wounds. And then I had to find the courage to address it and opt for separation and divorce. A truly huge amount of disturbing grace was needed to lead me along the spiral towards that place of clarity and decision, which led to the final destruction of everything that I had carefully built up as the foundation of my life—first my pastoral vocation, then my conception of faith, and finally my idealized beliefs about the family unit.

In this stage, grace acted as a heat source. What was frozen began to melt, and life began to move on and grow. Impulses, feelings and longings awakened, causing conflicts and tensions and revealing the weak artificiality that the system had painfully built to hide and repress them. Grace put together the conditions for life to be free again.

Grace wants growth and freedom. Nothing less. In their pursuit, grace may be fierce and demanding.

3. The Stage of Building a New Life Structure

This stage is partially intertwined with the previous. Making those difficult decisions, principally resigning from my job as a pastor and deciding to divorce, I faced the emptiness and desolation of my life, the inner life as much as the outer.

I had lost a job that was bringing me narcissistic gratification, even if at a very high cost. I was struggling to build a new career, with academic training and experience at the very least atypical and not fitting the average offers on the job market. I had lost almost all of my social network and friends and was discovering that it was not easy to find new ones. I was becoming more and more aware that my inner life, deprived of the reassuring presence of my rigid beliefs, was looking more like a desert than like a luxuriant jungle. And finally, I was finding myself alone in a little flat for the first time in my life.

During the years needed for that process of dismantling and reconstruction, grace manifested steadily in sustaining my courage and determination to find ways through. It created opportunities and chances at some crucial moments. Many times I felt like the universe was helping me. I found my first job, which gave me opportunities for on-the-job training and connections that opened the door for a second job, where I would find interesting work, a good salary, and the possibility of advancement. I began to meditate, to build new friendships, to cultivate my inner garden. Best of all, I met Evelise, with whom I would discover a level of connection and a quality of love and relationship that I couldn't have imagined before.

Thanks to her, I discovered Yoga, I dug deeper into meditation, I was challenged to dare to desire, to hope and to build. I began to enjoy for the first time dimensions of peace, happiness and ease, feeling loved and accepted. Our relationship became a place of security, where both of us could care for each other, and at the same time challenge one another to grow and mature, to be open to new life experiences and new depth of feelings. Meeting her has been the truest expression of grace in my life, for which I'll always be grateful.

This stage is where I began to experience grace as the healing and blessing power it is, sustaining life and bringing growth and freedom.

4. The Stage of Going Deeper and Facing the Shadows

But at this point, even with these beautiful new life experiences, I was still far away from the center of the spiral. The journey was about to take on new momentum.

I had laid the basic structures for a better life. I had more strength and energy to live each day in awareness, as opposed to just surviving until the next day. Before that, I had needed much of my energy to repress my feelings, to numb myself to my unhappiness and pain, and to bury my impulses and inner conflicts. Now that I was discovering some peace and happiness and reclaiming some of that life energy, I could see more clearly that I needed to go back to looking into my depths and allowing more healing and consciousness to penetrate into my inner life.

I was inspired by my dear wife, who had begun therapy with a very skilled therapist. I soon followed her example and, session after session, received the help I needed to dig deeper into my past and to discover more and more of the repressed inner traumas. All this work prepared the way for me to be able to go through the dramatic events that threatened my life and health, and to take full advantage of this spiritual experience with Jesus, in order to find my way to go on living and growing.

In this book I present some of the most important discoveries I made through this inner work. It's a journey that is neverending, a work that is always in progress, the adventure of a life. In it I have found and still find the resources to face and go through the most difficult and dramatic moments of my existence. I reclaimed my life force and received back my life energy as never before. I explored my inner territories and found in them wells of peace and springs of joy, luxuriant jungles, beautiful landscapes, spaciousness and light. I received healing and clarity. I became intimate with myself. I learned to take better care of me and to become truly kind to all those parts of me that were repressed and wounded. I reconnected with my deepest impulses and aspirations, as I started learning to feel my emotions and listen to my intuition. Among these aspirations, I reconciled with my strong interest for spirituality and with my longing for the Great Mystery that lies behind everything, the place of silence from which originates all reality.

Grace's Threefold Calling

The more grace is acknowledged and received, the less it has to manifest as hindering, putting up obstacles, bringing heat and chaos, fighting against our ways of tyrannizing ourselves, and the more it can show up as sustaining and strengthening.

Grace is always mysterious and surprising: you cannot control it or anticipate its actions. It doesn't enter into our plans and schedules; it is free in its essence.

But there is a pattern, or preoccupation, in all its actions. It presents to every human being a threefold calling:

A calling to reality

Grace fiercely calls us to find freedom from all the delusions we are trapped in that keep us away from reality. All the projections coming from our inner wounds, from our expectations, from our fears and hopes skew what's real. All our idealizations and fantasies color our view of past or present. The habitual distortions make us consider that raw reality is not enough.

Grace is committed to reality and can help us to let go of grandiose ideas about ourselves, our God, our mission, our destiny. Grace helps us to value the present moment, the simple pleasures of just being, loving and enjoying life. Through that we can find more true acceptance and love for reality.

A calling to inner rest

In reality, we find inner rest. That rest is a freedom from our internalized tyrannies, our imposed "missions" born from our inner critic or imposed by our lineage, parents, families, culture or religion—or by anything. Grace lets us be, just be, and helps us to discover that being is enough.

Just being is something we need to learn, and it may require hard work. But this work is nothing compared with the exhausting and always vain effort of trying to complete missions we didn't choose and can't control. Paradoxically, the work that happens in rest produces rest. In rest we learn to discover and enjoy grace. When we act from that place of rest, our actions become fruitful and adequate.

A calling to integration

In enjoying even partially the peace of just being and acting in the world from that place of rest, we learn to accept and embrace everything that we are—all of our emotions, our strengths and weaknesses, intuitions and impulses. We can see more clearly our inner places of light and shadows, what we are ashamed of and what we are proud of. Grace frees us from the need to numb or ignore some parts of ourselves, or repress them.

That is integration. And in that internal process, we discover along the way that we are fully part of, and in profound solidarity with, every other human being. We share the same lights and shadows and the same humanity. Grace prevents us from any idea of being better, of being apart, or of being separate or elected.

As you can see, I needed nothing less than reconsidering my whole life journey and my lifelong relationship with Jesus. I had to fully digest, appropriate and transform my religious and spiritual heritage, received from parents, the church I was attending, and Christian history. Through that process, my relationship with Jesus needed to go through a kind of radical alchemy to be refined and purified of all its component toxicities.

In this process I gained a personal wisdom and an experience that allows me to live better. It gave me access to practice a much healthier and more grounded spirituality than ever before in my life. The lesson I learned the hard way is that it's very dangerous to be naive about spirituality: it can be a wonderful support, a compass to find your way through life's struggles, a guide for growth. But when spirituality and religiosity meet unresolved wounds and immature expectations, as demonstrated in the first part of this book, the alliance can produce a vast amount of toxicity and morbid effects, individually and collectively.

Therefore, I want to conclude this book with some general thoughts about spirituality and the place it can take in our contemporary society as well as in our individual lives. I'll also offer some tips on how to live spiritually in a way that sustains growth and health, and how to avoid the traps that make it toxic.

EPILOGUE

TIPS FOR A NONTOXIC AND LIFE-SUSTAINING SPIRITUALITY

For many of us, our modern society is an environment in which it is difficult to have a sense of meaning for our existence and the place we occupy in the world. Our society is globalized, but we as individuals often feel atomized and sometimes lost and insignificant.

We can no longer count on the traditional institutions, roles, or models that helped our parents and grandparents find their place in the world and gave structure and direction to their lives. All of us must discover how to build our own personalities and values and chart the course of our lives.

We now have more precious autonomy and freedom than our ancestors could even imagine. But as we know, with autonomy comes choice, and freedom brings responsibility. Together they can be felt as a burden, confusing and destabilizing. They may become a source of anxiety, causing us to face the future as an apparently dangerous void, depending on life events and the difficulties we encounter.

In past traditional societies, spirituality was centrally important for structuring individuals and society, in the name of religious authority and of a god who was considered the guardian of social order. Religion, for the most part, has lost this function and its normative authority, and its monopoly on god has fortunately been broken. This opens a huge free space: for individuals, for women, and minorities. But it also creates an empty space, and emptiness may be frightening.

Nothing has been able to fill that void with the same structuring capacity, though many attempts have been made: not the welfare state, not science, not politics, not utopian social experiments, to name a few. Therefore it's tempting to renounce this freedom and to avoid the anxiety-inducing autonomy, and instead look for systems that seem to reintroduce the security, be it in an idealized or fantasized past, or in a present absolute authority that too often becomes totally abusive.

Some of this happened in the 70's and 80's with the widespread interest of many young people in cults and fringe religious movements. Today it shows up more in the universal and unfortunate return of the many stripes of fundamentalism. Muslim fundamentalism, of course, makes the headlines most often. But every religion and every culture today sees its manifestation in many forms, whether Catholic, Evangelical, Orthodox, Buddhist, Hindu.... the list goes on.

In this context we need to discover a free and healthy spirituality that embraces joyfully the reality of this time and the tremendous free space that we find before us. Because yes, the globalized women and men we have become truly need spirituality and inner life to find structure and support. Indeed, our life trajectories are often uncertain in an evolving environment, where the reference points are moving and the challenges numerous.

There are signs that this rediscovery is in the cards: I can feel it in the attraction of the public, as well as scientists and institutions, to meditation and yoga, to dialogue among religions, to silence, to integrative therapy and to mysticism.

What will characterize a spirituality that truly meets the particular challenges and needs of individuals and society at large? Because of my own experience, I'm mistrustful towards any form of fundamentalism. I want to promote for myself and for others a spirituality that takes advantage of the tremendous space of freedom opened up by the shock and the mix of cultures and currents of thought made possible by our ongoing globalization.

Here are some characteristics of such a spirituality:

- It draws on traditional sources but dares to reinterpret them, combine them and adapt them to the moment and its needs.
- At the same time, it draws on science and recent discoveries, and dares to evaluate them and enrich itself with these contributions.
- It leaves individuals free and responsible for their path and behavior, while giving them symbolic tools of meaning.
- It is integrative. It creates no separations or exclusions, but instead helps us to find our place in the moving environments in which we evolve, without rejecting other human beings or parts of ourselves.

Each of us needs to know our roots and heritage. For some it's Christianity, for others Islam, Buddhism, or laicity. Some have grown up in totally secular backgrounds and discovered spirituality through Yoga or meditation. In all cases, we need at some point to connect or reconnect with our heritage in a new and more conscious way, through refinement, purification and finally ownership of it. Such examination is the only way to identify and free ourselves from its toxic and oppressive components, and to reclaim any good and healthy parts.

As I said, it's very dangerous to be naive about spirituality and religion. They both can trap us into magical thinking, immaturity, rigidity, self-destructive behavior, or abuse of others. The only way to go through it and find the freedom we deserve and need is to evolve our consciousness, digging deep into our history, individual and collective, finding our traumas and tyrannies, and then addressing them. I hope this book has given you an illustration of this process and some keys for applying it to your own journey. I hope, too, that it gives you some hope and perspective of the beautiful discoveries and precious freedom that can be gained on this path, and the resources that a healthy spirituality can offer.

At a point in my life, I was thinking that Christianity was a closed chapter for me, or would only remain a marginal part of my spirituality, a place of some nostalgia and a lot of bad memories and experiences I had turned my back on. I was enjoying everything I was discovering in my new fields of practice and didn't consider ever going back to those roots. But I finally decided to do just that: go back to my roots, because in some way the dramatic circumstances I was going through brought me there, to grace and to a new lucidity. As a consequence, I now feel more grounded, more conscious and much richer. I discovered how much Christian mythology, archetypes, and representations are part of my DNA. And now that I went through this process of detoxification and purification, reconnecting with my heritage has allowed me to access the depths of practice that I never thought possible.

Before my amputation, I was teaching meditation and Yoga Nidra, in the two traditions of mindfulness and Yogic meditation. I look forward to coming back to that activity, as soon as I am able to. And I'm definitely not going to teach any kind of "Christian" meditation. I'm deeply convinced that meditation is a universal practice that has existed in different forms in all ancient religions and spiritual currents. Therefore, the practice of meditation must be offered to anybody interested in deepening her or his spirituality, whatever their religion or tradition. In fact, I see meditation as a necessary tool for the process of discovery, purification, and finally integration of one's religious and spiritual heritage, which is essential for any form of healthy spirituality.

To conclude, I propose three final questions to ask if you want to discern whether your spirituality is healthy and life-sustaining:

1. Is your spirituality or religion in service of your growth as a responsible and mature human being? Does it help you to evolve and face life challenges, to become more lucid and enjoy life? Does it challenge you to become more open-minded and able to listen to others, whatever their tribes, religions or traditions?

2. Do its tenets value your daily life, down to the simplest practical realities and relationships, moments of joys and pleasures, work, even pains and frustrations? Does it make all of this "mundane stuff" the opportunity par excellence for meeting the Divine or the Mystery, without any attempt to run away from it or devalue it?

3. Finally, is it rooted in the work of expanding your consciousness and dedicated to the healing of your traumas and inner wounds, instead of trying to justify or hide them? Is it walking hand in hand with a deep therapeutic work, encouraging and sustaining it when necessary? Does it help you to integrate with kindness and clarity every part of you, without rejecting any?

May these words contribute to your growth, healing and integration, in order to become a kinder, softer and more alive human being!

AFTERWORD
TWO YEARS LATER

Here I am two years after the tragedy. At the end of May, I went once more through my three-month scan and the MRI to find that no metastasis had reappeared. This is an important step that will allow me to space out these controls.

Tonight, I am hosting my weekly meditation course online, and just now, I have a counseling session via Skype with one of the clients who asks me to accompany them in the work of spiritual healing and deepening. I help them get rid of the toxic religious influences of their education. A fortnight ago, Evelise and I led a yoga and meditation retreat, which was a great experience for us as well as for the participants. In a few months, I will finish training as a hypnotherapist using cognitive and behavioral techniques.

I learn to walk with a prosthesis, a bulky robot leg that I attach to my hips with a plastic belt molded around my pelvis. I swim, meditate, and learn to treat myself with more tenderness and respect every day. And despite the handicap, with him, I feel more whole than ever.

I seize the opportunity of these upheavals to redirect my life toward the activities that are close to my heart. I reclaim with great joy the healthy part of my adolescent attraction towards the Great Mystery and towards others, enriched by this whole process and freed from constraints and guilt that once crushed and poisoned me.

I live one day at a time, aware as ever of the fragility of existence. The suffering, frustration, and reminder of my limits are daily by my side. Death and fear have become very concrete realities and sometimes remind me of their presence.

Yet, I have never been filled with such a vital impulse, full of projects, grateful for each moment and opportunity to learn, feel, and taste in the present moment. During this journey which continues day after day, I have gained courage, wisdom, lucidity, and above all a sense of my own dignity and the unique value of my existence.

I have just received from my editor the cover of this book, with a dark picture of the toxic Jesus. It makes me realize a little better that this book is really close to being realized. With all my heart, I wish that what I share will be a milestone for you and help you on your own journey towards yourself and your own way of receiving grace and freeing yourself from all of influences to which you have been exposed. I hope it helps you create a renewed connection with Reality and with the Great Mystery.

Marc-Henri Sandoz Paradella
Pully, July 2020
www.marchenrisandoz.com

ACKNOWLEDGMENTS

I recommend the following books that inspired me during my writing.

Bourgeault, C. (2010). *The Meaning of Mary Magdalene: Discovering the Woman at the Heart of Christianity*. Boston: Shambhala.

Bourgeault, C. (2016). *The Heart of Centering Prayer: Nondual Christianity in Theory and Practice*. Boulder: Shambhala.

Dupuche, J. R. (2005). *Jesus, the Mantra of God: An Exploration of Mantra Meditation*. Melbourne: David Lovell.

Keating, T. (2014). *Reflections on the Unknowable*. New York: Lantern Books.

Mabry, J. R. (2015). *The Monster God: Coming to Terms with the Dark Side of Divinity*. Berkeley: The Apocryphile Press.

Main, J. (2007). *The Gethsemane Talks: Christian Meditation: A Simple Teaching on Meditation in the Christian Tradition*. Singapore: Medio Media.

Marion, J. (2004). *The Death of the Mythic God: the Rise of Evolutionary Spirituality*. Newburyport: Hampton Roads Publishing.

Masters, R. A. (2013). *Emotional Intimacy: A Comprehensive*

Guide for Connecting with the Power of Your Emotions. Boulder: Sounds True.

Masters, R. A. (2014). *Spiritual Bypassing: When Spirituality Disconnects Us from What Really Matters*. Berkeley, Calif.: North Atlantic Books.

McLaren, B. D. (2017). *Great Spiritual Migration*. Hodder & Stoughton.

Miller, R. (2010). *Yoga Nidra: A Meditative Practice for Deep Relaxation and Healing*. Boulder: Sounds True.

Sardello, R., Sanders-Sardello, C., Sheker-Schroeder, T., & Overdrive Inc. (2011). *Silence: The Mystery of Wholeness*. North Atlantic Books.

Smith, P. R. (2011). *Integral Christianity: The Spirit's Call to Evolve*. St. Paul: Paragon House Publishers.

Made in the USA
Middletown, DE
09 April 2021